Chameleon Quilts

Margrit Hall

©2006 Margrit Hall
Published by

kp **krause publications**
An Imprint of F+W Publications

700 East State Street • Iola, WI 54990-0001
715-445-2214 • 888-457-2873

Our toll-free number to place an order or obtain
a free catalog is (800) 258-0929.

Library of Congress Catalog Number: 2006931557

ISBN-13: 978-0-89689-384-9
ISBN-10: 0-89689-384-7

Edited by Susan Sliwicki and Andy Belmas
Interior design by Sandy Kent

Printed in China

DEDICATIONS

With love to my husband and best friend David, for his love, help and support.

To my children Valerie, Robyn and Eric and my grandchildren, especially 9-year-old Hailey, who sat by my side while I sewed and took out all my pins.

To Earlene Fowler for her friendship, inspiration, and encouragement.

ACKNOWLEDGMENTS

A very special thank you for two wonderful friends, Rhoda Nelson and Cathryn Tallman-Evans, who always came to my aid whenever I needed help and to Mary Tabar who generously gave of her time.

I want to sincerely thank all of the wonderful quilters who made my quilts better with their incredible talent: Ginger Hayes, Ginny Jaranowski, Phyllis Reddish and Vicki Stratton.

Thank you to all the wonderful people at Krause Publications, especially Candy Wiza in helping to make this book a reality.

A huge thank you to Susan Sliwicki and Andy Belmas, whose editorial expertise and thoughtful insights have made this book everything I had hoped it would be.

A very special thank you to Francie Ginocchio for all of her technical expertise.

Thank you to Superior Threads for the contribution of thread for all of the quilts and projects and to Hoffman California Fabrics, RJR Fabrics and Robert Kaufman Fabrics for their donations of the fabric used in this book.

Note: Fabrics used in the quilts shown may not currently be available.

FOREWORD

It's hard to say what first attracted me to Margrit Hall's quilts, her extravagant and exciting use of color or her striking, innovative designs. All I knew at first glance was that they spoke to something deep inside me. She has a unique talent for taking traditional patterns, which have always intrigued me, and turning them on their side to create a look that both gives homage to the old and celebrates the new.

When we met, Margrit and I found we had a lot in common besides our love for quilts and a somewhat quirky sense of humor. In her I found a creative sister, one who desired as I did to work within the boundaries of her chosen artistic field, yet bring to it something new, something of her own. It amazed me as we worked together how she saw things, so differently from me as a writer, yet so much the same. Like a writer uses words to create pictures and elicit emotions in a reader, Margrit uses color, texture and shape to do the very same thing. The difference is Margrit's creations can also keep you warm on a cold winter night!

I know you will love Margrit's quilts in this book and will enjoy how much fun she makes designing patterns. She is a wonderful teacher, as well as artist. If I had a quarter for every person I met as we toured together who said, "Margrit Hall was my first quilt teacher", I'd be able to buy that ranch I've always wanted. This book is as good as one of her delightful quilting classes. Have a great time!

Earlene Fowler
Author of the "Benni Harper Quilt Mysteries"

TABLE *of* CONTENTS

How-to
Quilting
Basics

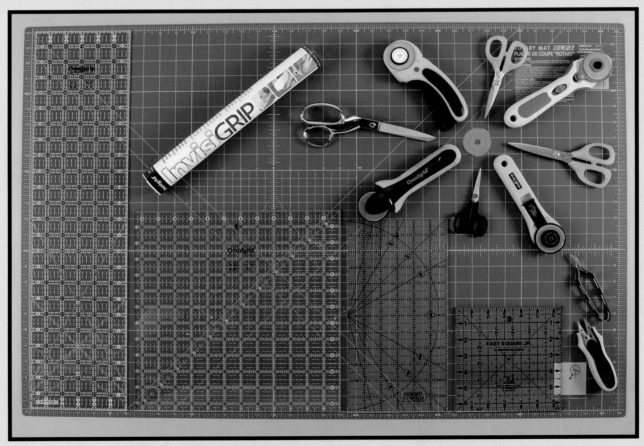

Before you get started, it's a good idea to familiarize yourself with tools,
fabrics and techniques you'll need to complete the projects.

Fabric Basics

All fabric strips are cut on the crosswise grain width of fabric unless instructed otherwise. All fabric requirements are based on 42"-wide fabric. Fabric widths may vary and fabric may shrink when washed. After cutting strips, carefully trim selvages.

If you like a strong contrast in your quilt, use a complementary color scheme. Complementary colors are two colors that are exactly opposite each other on the color wheel. When complementary colors such as blue and orange or yellow and purple are used together, the colors appear to vibrate and add life to the quilt.

Prewashing Fabric

There are advantages and disadvantages to prewashing fabric. Washing will preshrink the fabric and remove excess dye. Fabrics can become limp and lose body when they are prewashed. Using spray starch when you press the fabric after prewashing can restore some of the body. To be safe, check the fabric for color fastness by thoroughly wetting a small area or fabric scrap and pressing it between two pieces of white fabric. If the color transfers to the white fabric, you should probably prewash. If you decide to prewash, be sure to include all of the fabric used in that project.

Pressing

Unless otherwise stated, seams in the projects are pressed in the direction of the pressing arrows in the diagrams. On occasion, seams may be pressed open. Press on the right side of the fabric to ensure the project will lay flat with no puckers. Whenever possible, alternate direction of seams to eliminate bulky areas.

Tools

Accurate measuring, marking and cutting are vital to the success of your finished project. For the projects in this book, you will need the following tools:

- Sharp rotary cutter
- Cutting mat
- Hard plastic ruler at least 6" x 12" (see Resources)
- 15" x 15" Omnigrid Ruler for cutting fabric is recommended, but optional cutting directions are given
- See-through template plastic for making the templates
- ¼" bias bar for constructing appliqué vines
- 3½" finished quarter circle template (Elisa's Backporch, see Resources) for making some of the Drunkard's Path Quilts in Chapter 6. Templates for quilts are provided.

Additional general quilting tools that are mentioned in this book and that may prove helpful as you create:

- Sharp scissors that are used only for fabric
- Thread, gray tones for general construction, as they blend well with most fabrics
- Thread, matching fabrics for binding
- Iron
- Pressing sheet for fusible web appliqué
- Straight pins made for quilting projects
- Sharp pencil for marking and tracing
- Chalk for marking
- Basting glue
- T-Pins to hold quilt layers in place on carpeting
- Milliner's needles for hand basting layers
- Curved safety pins for pin basting layers
- Rotary cutting blades become dull and mats do wear out as grooves are cut into them. Replace blades and mats as needed to keep tools sharp for accurate cutting.

CUTTING, PIECING AND SEWING

Seam Allowances

Accurate cutting and stitching is essential for a great finished result. A ¼" seam allowance is used for all projects unless otherwise noted.

To determine your sewing accuracy, try the following ¼" seam allowance test.

1. Cut four strips of fabric, 2" x 6½", and sew the strips together lengthwise.
2. Press the seams (on right side as stated above) in one direction.

The block should be square and measure 6½" x 6½". If the block is larger, the seam allowance is too narrow. If the block is smaller, the seam allowance is too wide. Adjust your seam allowance accordingly.

← 6½" →

6½"

If this measurement is not equal to 6½" then adjust your seam allowance.

Sewing Strip Sets

When constructing strip sets, sew strips together lengthwise. Since fabrics are of different lengths, trim the ends of the strip sets before cutting into squares or segments.

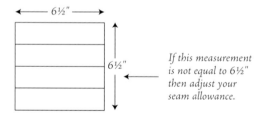

TIP When cutting squares, rectangles and triangles, first cut strips as indicated in the cutting instructions for each project.

Quick Piece-and-Trim Basics

I like to use a combination of quick piecing and trimming. A quick method for piecing half-square triangles is to layer two fabrics, right sides together, and mark squares on the wrong side of the top fabric. Mark a diagonal line through each square and stitch ¼" on each side of the line. Cut on the marked line, and press the units open. You now have two half-square triangles. Sizes are calculated so that you can place a square template or see-through ruler on top of the pieced units and trim them to the desired project size. The following chart is an example showing how to calculate half- and quarter-square triangles.

Half-Square Triangles
Add ⅞" to the finished length of the triangle's short side.

Finished Side = 4"
4" + ⅞" = 4⅞"
Block Finished Size + ⅞" = Size of Square

Quarter-Square Triangles
Add 1¼" to the finished length of the triangle's long side.

Finished Side = 4"
4" + 1¼" = 5¼"
Block Finished Size + 1¼" = Size of Square

1/8	= .125
1/4	= .25
3/8	= .375
1/2	= .50
5/8	= .625
3/4	= .75
7/8	= .875

Decimal Conversion Chart

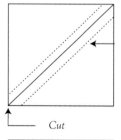

Cut

Sew

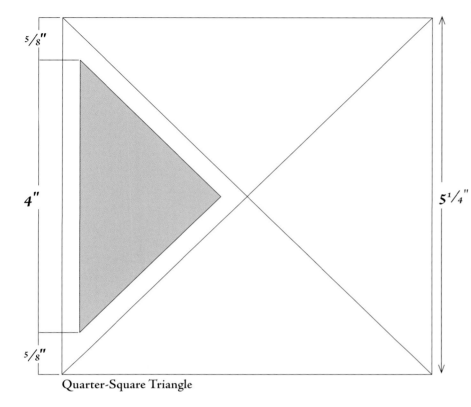

5/8"

4"

5/8"

5¼"

Quarter-Square Triangle

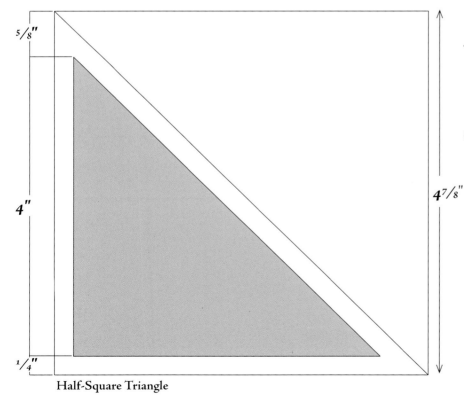

5/8"

4"

1/4"

4⅞"

Half-Square Triangle

Fusible Web Appliqué

1. Lay the fusible web, paper side up, on the reversed pattern and trace with a pencil. NOTE: Reverse appliqué patterns are used for projects in this book that are not symmetrical. If you choose to hand appliqué, you must flip the pattern over. Leave approximately ½" between each appliqué.

2. Cut out appliqués, leaving a small border of paper around each piece.

3. Following the manufacturer's directions, iron the fusible side of the web to the wrong side of the appliqué fabric. Using an appliqué pressing sheet will help keep the adhesive from sticking to your iron.

4. Cut out on the pencil line. Remove the paper and using manufacturer's directions press appliqué in place, fusible side down.

5. Machine or hand sew a buttonhole stitch around the appliqué. Use your choice of matching, contrasting, or invisible thread.

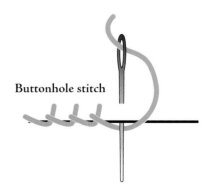

Buttonhole stitch

Bias Strips Using Bias Bars

1. To make the bias strips for appliqué vines, fold the squares on the diagonal. Follow cutting directions to ensure the square used to make the bias is a perfectly square piece. Cut off the fold, then cut into 1"-wide bias strips.

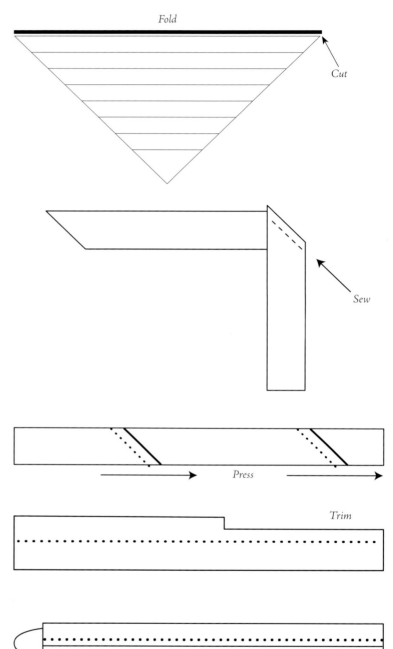

Fold

Cut

2. Lay bias strips right sides together, perpendicular to each other, and sew, using a ¼" seam allowance. Press all seams in one direction. This will allow the bias bar to slide through the tube without catching any seam. Continue to join enough strips to reach desired length. The corner and end pieces near the point may be too short to use for bias strips.

Sew

3. Sew strips together.

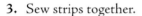

Press

4. Fold strips in half lengthwise, right sides out. Stitch ¼" from the folded edge. Trim the seam allowance close to the stitching.

Trim

5. Insert a ¼" bias bar (found in local quilt and fabric stores or see Resources) into the bias tube. Roll the seam to the center of the bar. Press as you slide the bias bar through the inside of the tube, centering the seam on the back of the bar.

TIP Make sure to insert the bar so it passes through the tube in the same direction that the piecing seams are pressed.

BORDERS

The borders used for the projects in this book are called butted borders, also known as straight sewn borders. The top and bottom borders are usually sewn on first, then the side borders are cut (sometimes sewn to corner units) and sewn along the quilt sides, including the top and bottom borders.

When the quilt top is finished, measure the quilt horizontally across the center. Cut the top and bottom borders to fit this measurement. Sew the borders to the top and bottom of the quilt. Press the seams toward the borders.

Next, measure the quilt vertically through the center, including the top and bottom borders. Cut the side borders to fit this measurement, and sew the borders to the sides of the quilt.

If the border measurement is less than 42", only one strip for each side is needed. If the border measurement is between 42" and 63", one-and-one-half strips are needed. To make a one-and-one-half strip, cut a 42" strip in half widthwise and sew the 21" strip end to end with the 42" strip, as illustrated below.

If the border measurement is between 63" and 84", sew two 42" strips together end to end. It may be more visually pleasing if the seam is not directly in the center of the border, so if possible, offset the seam placement.

TIP Instead of cutting border strips the exact length, place a pin at the correct length and cut slightly longer. Trim to the correct size after the border is sewn to the quilt. Example: If the quilt measures 38½", cut the strip 42" and pin the strip at the 38½" mark.

TIP For perfect narrow borders, cut border ¼" wider than desired measurement. Example: If a 1¼" strip is required, cut a 1½"-wide strip.

Sew borders to top and bottom of the quilt. Lay a ruler on the seam line at the finished measurement plus ¼". Example: If the border finishes at ½" wide, trim the border to measure ¾". This method will give a straight and accurate edge to attach the next border.

NOTE: When using this method, add ⅛ yard to the fabric requirement for that fabric.

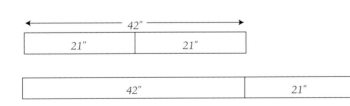

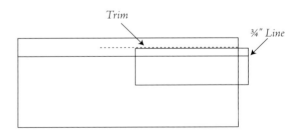

FINISHING

Backing

1. The fabric you choose for your quilt backing should be at least 2" larger on each side than the quilt top. (If using a long-arm machine for quilting, the backing should be at least 4" larger).

2. Trim off selvages and piece your backing to the correct size.

3. For a patchwork look, use the leftover fabric in your fabric stash to piece your backing.

Batting

Batting is truly a personal preference. For wall hangings, or for a softer, antique look, use a lightweight cotton or cotton blend. For a fluffier look, use a light- or medium-weight polyester. Cut batting at least 2" to 4" larger than your quilt top on each side.

Layering

Lay the backing wrong side up on a large table or on the floor, and tape the edges with masking tape. Make sure the backing is stretched flat. If you are working on a carpeted surface, use T-Pins to hold the backing to the carpet. Center the batting on top of the backing. Center the quilt top right side up on top of the batting and backing; then smooth out any wrinkles.

Basting

For machine quilting, baste the layers together using 1" or 2" long safety pins (or curved safety pins made specially for pin basting). For hand quilting, baste the layers together using a long needle (I like milliner's needles since they gently bend), contrasting thread and long stitches.

Begin your pin or thread basting in the quilt center and work toward the outer edges of the quilt. Baste in vertical rows, then in horizontal rows, 3" to 4" apart.

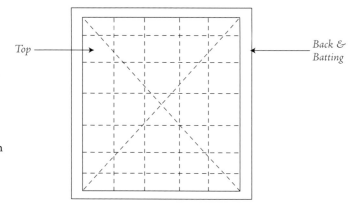

Top → ← Back & Batting

To prevent the outer edges and layers from shifting as you apply the binding, baste ⅛" from the outside edges of the quilt. If you are machine basting, I recommend using a walking foot to control any fabric shifting and to prevent tucks.

QUILTING

Quilting can be done either by hand or machine. Quilting can be functional by holding the layers together, and it can also be decorative by enhancing or embellishing the design of your quilt top. Many quilting designs and stencils are available, or you can design your own. You can find many professional quilters available to quilt your projects. Check with your local quilt shop or guild for a list of area quilters who specialize in hand or machine (even free motion) quilting.

Straight-Grain, Double-Fold Binding

1. Trim the extra batting and backing from the quilt. Stitch ⅛" from the outside edges around the entire quilt. This will keep the layers from shifting as you are sewing on the binding.
2. For ¼"-wide finished binding, cut 2¼"-wide strips from the crosswise width of the fabric. Sew strips together using diagonal seams. Place strips, right sides together, with ends at right angles. Draw a line from A to B. Sew on the dotted line and cut on the solid line. Press seams open. Continue sewing strips together to make a continuous

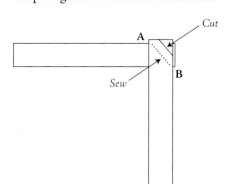

binding strip that will edge the perimeter of the quilt. Use a matching thread and small stitch when sewing binding strips together so stitching does not show.

3. Lay a 45-degree angle ruler on the starting end of the binding, and trim.
4. Fold the strips in half lengthwise, wrong sides together, and press the entire length of the strip. With raw edges together, and starting a least 6" from a corner of the quilt, pin the binding to one side of the quilt. Make sure to leave the first 3" to 4" of the binding unattached. Sew the binding to the quilt using a ¼" seam allowance. Sew to ¼" from the first corner, and backstitch.

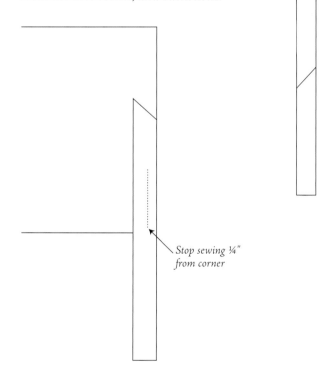

Trim

45°

*Stop sewing ¼"
from corner*

5. Fold the binding strip at a right angle so it extends upward and is even with the second side of the quilt.

— Fold

6. Fold the binding down even with the second side of the quilt. Make sure the top fold is even with the first quilt side. Begin sewing at the top and sew to ¼" from the next corner. Repeat.

6"

3"- 4"

7. To finish binding, continue sewing binding to 6" from the beginning of the binding. Remove the quilt from the machine. Open the binding fold.

8. Lay the quilt on a flat surface and place the right binding tail over the left binding tail. Where they intersect, draw a 45-degree angle on the left tail.

9. Measure ½" from the drawn line, and draw a line parallel to the first line. Cut off the excess binding.

Cut

½"

10. Join the ends together with a diagonal seam, press seam open and refold the binding in half. Finish sewing the binding to the quilt. Turn the binding to the backside of the quilt, pin in place and stitch to the back by hand with matching thread.

THE RAIL FENCE

These Rail Fence quilts have the same basic pattern, but the different fabrics and block sizes give them very unique looks. Vary the quilt by using more rails or more light and dark contrast in each block to create an entirely different feel!

Finished Quilt: 36¾" x 47¼"   Finished Block: 5¼"

SMALL BABY QUILT

For the Small Baby Quilt, I use what I call a "hidden color." By using red in the inner border and the corner stars, the red hidden colors in the print fabrics become points of interest to the eye. And, three shades each of yellow and blue fabric adds colorful variety.

Materials

½ yd. yellow fabric 1
¼ yd. yellow fabric 2
¼ yd. yellow fabric 3
¼ yd. blue fabric 1
¼ yd. blue fabric 2
¼ yd. blue fabric 3
⅜ yd. red fabric
¾ yd. large blue print
⅜ yd. blue print
1½ yd. backing
43" x 53" batting
Sewing tools and supplies

Fabric	Cut	For
Yellow 1	1 strip. Cut into 16 squares, 2" x 2"	Outer border corner units
Yellow 1	2 strips. Cut into 16 squares, 2⅝" x 2⅝"	Outer border corner units
Yellow 1, 2 and 3	3 strips each, 2¼" wide	Rail 2, 1 and 3
Blue 1, 2 and 3	3 strips each, 2¼" wide	Rail 1, 2 and 3
Red	4 strips, 1¼" wide	Inner border
Red	2 strips. Cut into 16 squares, 2⅝" x 2⅝"	Outer border corner units
Red	Remaining strip into 4 squares, 2" x 2"	Outer border corner units
Large blue print	4 strips, 5" wide	Outer border
Blue print	5 strips, 2¼" wide	Binding

Block Construction

1. Sew one each of the three blue print 2¼"-wide strips together. Make three sets as illustrated, and press in the direction of the arrows.
2. Measure the width of the sets (should be 5¾") and cut sets into 18 squares, 5¾" x 5¾".
3. Repeat for yellow rail fabrics (make 17 yellow squares).

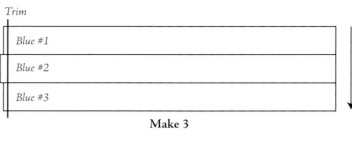

Make 3

Quilt Assembly

Arrange the quilt pieces as illustrated, with 7 rows of 5 blocks each. Alternate the 18 blue and 17 yellow squares. Blues are vertical blocks and yellows are horizontal. Sew blocks together and press toward the yellow squares.

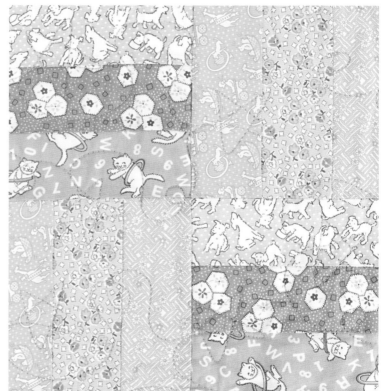

Corner Unit Construction

1. Draw a diagonal line across the back of the 2⅝" yellow squares. Place four of the 2⅝" yellow squares, right sides together, with four red 2⅝" squares. Sew ¼" from each side of the drawn line. Cut on the drawn diagonal line. Open the squares and press. Using a 2" square template, trim blocks to 2".

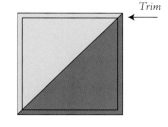

2. Sew a yellow 2" square to two sides of a red and yellow half-square block; press toward the arrows. Make 2.

Make 2

3. Sew a 2" red and yellow half-square block to two sides of a 2" red square.

4. Sew together to make a Pinwheel Corner Block. Repeat for a total of 4 blocks.

Make 4

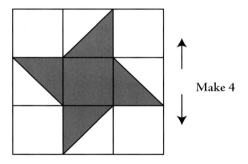

Borders

NOTE: *Refer to Borders section in How-to Quilting Basics for detailed border instructions.*

INNER BORDER

NOTE: For the inner border, see the Hint for Perfect Narrow Borders in How-to Quilting Basics.

1. Measure, cut and sew two of the 1¼"-wide red strips to the top and bottom of the quilt.
2. Repeat for the sides of the quilt.

OUTER BORDER

1. Measure and cut two of the 5"-wide blue print strips to fit the top and bottom of the quilt. Do not sew to the quilt.
2. Measure and cut two of the 5"-wide blue print strips to fit the sides of the quilt. Sew the corner units to each end of the side border strips.
3. Sew the top and bottom borders to the quilt. Sew the side borders with the corner units to the sides of the quilt.

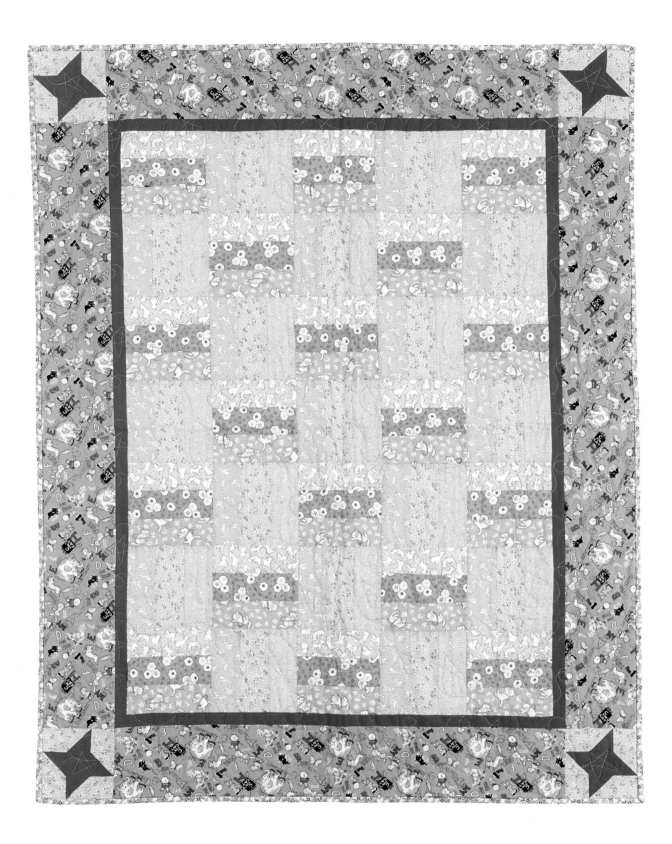

CRAZY COLOR QUILT

For this fun lap quilt, I started with a fabric that I found interesting and decided to use it as the border print. I then selected the blue and orange fabrics to coordinate with the border. Since there was black within the fabrics, I chose black as the hidden color.

Finished Quilt: 45½" x 57¼"   **Finished Block:** 6"

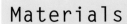

Materials

½ yd. blue fabric
¼ yd. blue fabric 1
¼ yd. blue fabric 2
¼ yd. blue fabric 3
¼ yd. blue fabric 4
⅝ yd. orange fabric
¼ yd. orange fabric 1
¼ yd. orange fabric 2
¼ yd. orange fabric 3
¼ yd. orange fabric 4
¼ yd. black fabric
⅜ yd. multi fabric
1 yd. large multi fabric
½ yd. binding
2¾ yd. backing
52" x 63" batting
Sewing tools and supplies

Fabric	Cut	For
Blue	6 strips, 2½" x 21"	Rails
Blue	2 strips. Cut into 8 squares, 3⅛" x 3⅛"	Outer border corner units
Blue	Remaining strip into 4 squares, 2½" x 2½"	Outer border corner units
Blue 1, 2, 3 and 4	6 strips each, 2½" x 21"	Rails
Orange	2 strips. Cut into 8 squares, 3⅛" x 3⅛"	Outer border corner units
Orange	1 strip. Cut into 16 squares, 2½" x 2½"	Outer border corner units
Orange 1, 2, 3 and 4	6 strips each, 2½" x 21"	Rails
Black	5 strips, 1" wide	Inner border
Multi	5 strips, 1¾" wide	Middle border
Large multi	5 strips, 6½" wide	Outer border
Binding	6 strips, 2¼" wide	

Block Construction

1. Sew the blue half strips (2½" x 21") together, making 10 sets with different combinations of blue prints. Cut each set into three blocks, 6½" x 6½". You'll have more blocks than needed, but this method provides a wider variety of print combinations.
2. Repeat with orange fabrics, making 8 sets.

Quilt Assembly

Arrange the quilt pieces as illustrated for the Small Baby Quilt, with seven rows of five blocks each. Alternate the 18 blue and 17 orange squares. Blues are vertical blocks and oranges are horizontal. Sew blocks together and press toward the orange squares.

Corner Unit Construction

Using 3⅛" orange and blue squares, make half-square blocks. Using a 2½" square template or a small quilter's ruler, trim blocks to 2½". Piece the blocks as illustrated for the Small Baby Quilt.

Borders

NOTE: *Refer to Borders section in How-to Quilting Basics for detailed border instructions.*

INNER BORDER

Note: *See the Hint for Perfect Narrow Borders in How-to Quilting Basics.*

1. Measure, cut and sew two of the 1½"-wide black strips to the top and bottom of the quilt.
2. Repeat for the sides of the quilt, using three strips to piece borders for needed length.

MIDDLE BORDER

1. Repeat Step 1 for Inner Border, using the 1¾"-wide multi-print strips.
2. Repeat Step 2 for Inner Border.

OUTER BORDER

1. Measure and cut two of the 6½"-wide large multi-print strips to fit the top and bottom of the quilt. Do not sew to the quilt.
2. Measure and cut three of the 6½"-wide large multi-print strips to fit the sides of the quilt, piecing strips for needed length. Sew the corner units to each end of the side border strips.
3. Sew the top and bottom borders to the quilt. Sew the side borders with the corner units to the sides of the quilt.

Finishing

Layer, quilt and bind. Refer to Finishing section in How-to Quilting
Basics for detailed instructions.

FOUR RAIL QUILT

This striking quilt has increased dimension and texture with the addition of the fourth rail. The appliquéd vines are a special treat, creating the perfect finishing touch.

Finished Quilt: 40" x 52"   Finished Block: 6"

Materials

¼ yd. blue fabric 1, 2, 3 and 4
⅜ yd. red fabric 1, 2, 3 and 4
1 yd. dark blue fabric
⅝ yd. green fabric
¼ yd. black fabric
⅜ yd. multi fabric
1 yd. large multi fabric
½ yd. red for binding
1⅝ yd. backing
1 yd. fusible web
46" x 58" batting
Sewing tools and supplies

TIP Instead of using templates to draw flower centers, use a coin or button to draw centers.

Fabric	Cut	For
Blue 1, 2, 3 and 4	3 strips each, 2" wide	Rails
Red 1, 2, 3 and 4	3 strips each, 2" wide	Rails
Red 1, 2 and 3	3 strips, 2" wide. Cut into 24 flowers using Template A (8 of each color)	Flowers
Red 4 (lightest)	3 strips, 2" wide. Cut into 8 flower centers using Template B	Flower centers
Dark blue	5 strips, 5½" wide	Border
Green	1 square, 19" x 19"	Vines
Green	1 square, 19" x 19". Cut into 24 leaves using Template C	Leaves
Red	5 strips, 2¼" wide	Binding

NOTE: *Before cutting appliqués, refer to Fusible Web Appliqué directions in How-to Quilting Basics.*

Block Construction

1. Sew 2"-wide strips of each of the four red fabrics (arranged in random order) together to make a strip set. Repeat to make three red strip sets. Cut sets into 6½" segments for a total of 17 segments.
2. Repeat with the four blue fabrics, making 18 blue segments.

6½"			
1			
2			
3			
4			

Press

Make 3 blue sets & orange sets
Cut 18 blue segments & 17 orange segments

Quilt Assembly

Arrange the quilt pieces as illustrated for the Small Baby Quilt, with seven rows of five blocks each. Alternate the 18 blue and 17 red blocks. Blues are vertical blocks and reds are horizontal. Sew blocks together and press toward the red blocks.

Borders

NOTE: *Refer to Borders section in How-to Quilting Basics for detailed border instructions.*

1. Measure, cut and sew two of the 5½"-wide dark blue strips to the top and bottom of the quilt.
2. Repeat for the sides of the quilt, using three strips to piece borders for needed length.

Appliqué

NOTE: *Refer to Fusible Web Appliqué and Bias Strips directions in How-to Quilting Basics.*

1. Fold the 19" green square on the diagonal and cut 1"-wide bias strips for appliqué vine.
2. Using the photo for placement, pin or baste the vine to the 5½" border (basting glue can be used). Stitch. Vine ends are trimmed and hidden under the corner flowers.
3. Using the fusible web appliqué method, fuse the flowers and leaves to the 5½"-wide border. Refer to the photo for placement. Hand or machine sew buttonhole stitch around the appliqué with black thread.

TIP If you like to embellish and add dimension to your quilts, buttons can be used for flower centers.

Finishing

Layer, quilt and bind. Refer to Finishing section in How-to Quilting
Basics for detailed instructions.

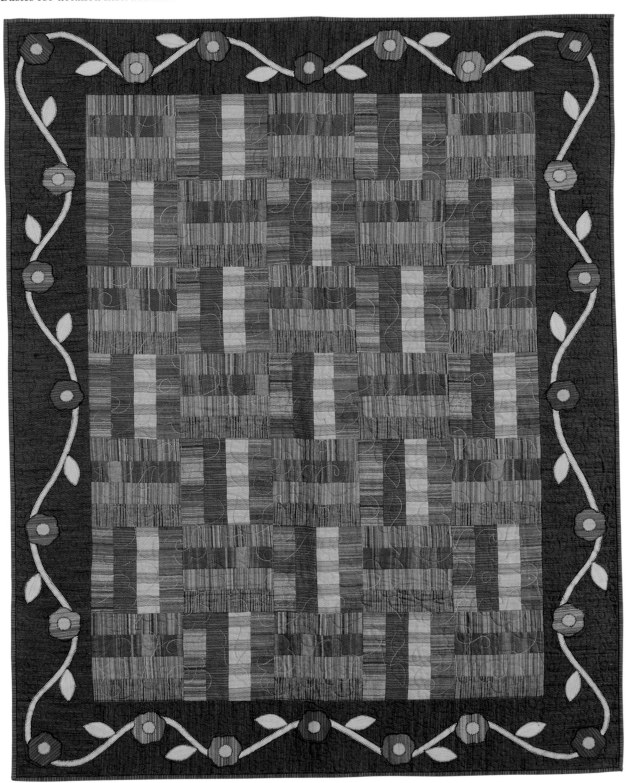

3

LOG CABIN

The Log Cabin is an all-time favorite quilt pattern. It's quick and easy to construct and offers a wide variety of layout design options. By changing fabrics and layout, you can go from a traditional country feel to a bright contemporary look.

Finished Quilt: 50½" x 68½"   Finished Block: 9"

COUNTRY SUNFLOWERS QUILT

The Country Sunflowers Quilt is set in a barn raising pattern. By using darker fabrics in the outer two rails, a secondary design is created.

Materials

¼ yd. red fabric
¼ yd. tan fabric
¼ yd. turquoise fabric
⅜ yd. gold fabric
⅜ yd. medium blue fabric
½ yd. medium brown fabric
⅜ yd. medium dark blue fabric
⅝ yd. dark brown fabric
2 yd. dark blue fabric
⅝ yd. dark green fabric
½ yd. light green fabric
⅜ yd. golden yellow fabric
3⅛ yd. backing
2 yd. fusible web
57" x 75" yd. batting
Sewing tools and supplies

Fabric	Cut	For
Red	24 squares, 1½" wide x 1½"	Centers
Red	5 strips, 1¾" wide	Inner border
Tan	8 flower centers using Template C	Flower centers
Tan	24 squares, 1½" wide x 1½"	Log 1
Tan	24 rectangles, 1½" wide x 2½"	Log 2
Turquoise	24 rectangles, 1½" wide x 2½"	Log 3
Turquoise	24 rectangles, 1½" wide x 3½"	Log 4
Gold	24 rectangles, 1½" wide x 3½"	Log 5
Gold	24 rectangles, 1½" wide x 4½"	Log 6
Medium blue	24 rectangles, 1½" wide x 4½"	Log 7
Medium blue	24 rectangles, 1½" wide x 5½"	Log 8
Medium brown	24 rectangles, 1½" wide x 5½"	Log 9
Medium brown	24 rectangles, 1½" wide x 6½"	Log 10
Medium dark blue	24 rectangles, 1½" wide x 6½"	Log 11
Medium dark blue	24 rectangles, 1½" wide x 7½"	Log 12
Dark brown	8 large flower centers using Template B	Large sunflower centers
Dark brown	24 rectangles, 1½" wide x 7½"	Log 13
Dark brown	24 rectangles, 1½" wide x 8½"	Log 14
Dark blue	24 rectangles, 1½" wide x 8½"	Log 15
Dark blue	24 rectangles, 1½" wide x 9½"	Log 16
Dark blue	6 strips, 6½" wide	Outer border
Dark blue	7 strips, 2¼" wide	Binding
Dark green	2 squares, 20" x 20"	Vine
Light green	32 leaves using Template D	Sunflower leaves
Golden yellow	8 flower petals using Template A	Sunflower petals

Construction directions to follow on page 34.

NOTE: *Before cutting appliqué pieces, refer to Fusible Web Appliqué section in How-to Quilting Basics.*

Finished Quilt: 49½" x 67½"   Finished Block: 9"

JEWEL TONE QUILT

The Jewel Tone Quilt flows by carrying one of the colors forward from the previous rail to the next. In this quilt, I carried pink, purple, green and teal forward. This technique allows a smooth transition from one color to another.

Materials

⅜ yd. bright pink print fabric
¼ yd. multi-print fabric
⅜ yd. purple fabric
½ yd. purple and teal fabric
⅝ yd. teal fabric
3⅛ yd. black fabric
3⅛ yd. backing
56" x 74" batting
Sewing tools and supplies

Fabric	Cut	For
Bright pink fabric	24 squares, 1½" wide x 1½", 5 strips, 1¼" wide	Centers and middle border
Multi	24 squares, 1½" wide x 1½"	Log 1
Multi	24 rectangles, 1½" wide x 2½"	Log 2
Purple	24 rectangles, 1½" wide x 3½"	Log 5
Purple	24 rectangles, 1½" wide x 4½"	Log 6
Purple and teal	24 rectangles, 1½" wide x 5½"	Log 9
Purple and teal	24 rectangles, 1½" wide x 6½"	Log 10
Teal	24 rectangles, 1½" wide x 7½"	Log 13
Teal	24 rectangles, 1½" wide x 8½"	Log 14
Black	24 rectangles, 1½" wide x 2½"	Log 3
Black	24 rectangles, 1½" wide x 3½"	Log 4
Black	24 rectangles, 1½" wide x 4½"	Log 7
Black	24 rectangles, 1½" wide x 5½"	Log 8
Black	24 rectangles, 1½" wide x 6½"	Log 11
Black	24 rectangles, 1½" wide x 7½"	Log 12
Black	24 rectangles, 1½" wide x 8½"	Log 15
Black	24 rectangles, 1½" wide x 9½"	Log 16
Black	5 strips, 1½" wide	Inner borders
Black	6 strips, 5½" wide	Outer borders

Log Cabin Block Construction

NOTE: *When the first light and first dark fabrics have been sewn around the center, you have completed one round. Blocks have four rounds.*

1. With right sides together, sew Log 1 to the center square. Press seams away from the center of the block.

2. Turning the block in a counterclockwise direction, sew on the remaining logs in sequence as illustrated, continuing to turn the block between logs. Make 24 blocks.

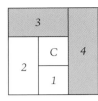

1st Round Completed

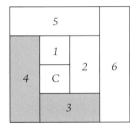

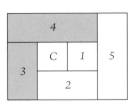

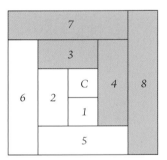

2nd Round Completed

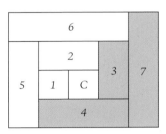

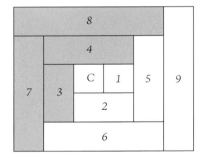

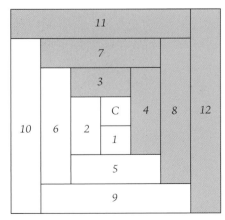

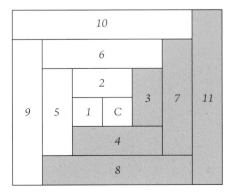

3rd Round Completed

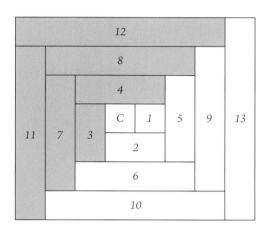

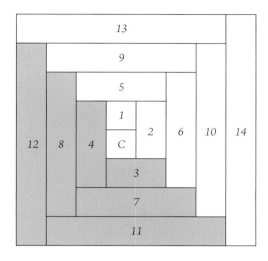

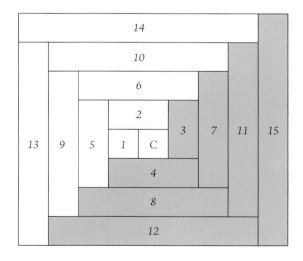

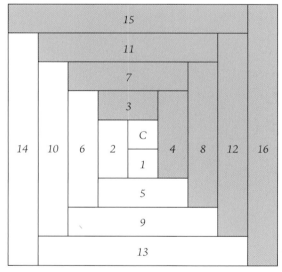

4th Round, Completed Block

Quilt Assembly

COUNTRY SUNFLOWERS QUILT

Arrange the quilt pieces in a Barn Raising pattern, using the photo and diagram as a guide.

JEWEL TONE QUILT

Arrange the quilt pieces in a Sunshine and Shadows pattern, using the photo and diagram as a guide.

Barn Raising

Sunshine and Shadows

Borders

Note: *Refer to Borders section in How-to Quilting Basics for detailed border instructions.*

COUNTRY SUNFLOWERS QUILT INNER BORDER

1. Measure, cut and sew two of the 1¾"-wide red strips to the top and bottom of the quilt.
2. Repeat for the sides of the quilt, using remaining strips to piece borders for needed length.

OUTER BORDER

1. Repeat Step 1 for Inner Border, using the 6½"-wide dark blue strips.
2. Repeat Step 2 for Inner Border.
3. Using the color photo for placement, prepare and appliqué the vine, leaves and sunflower to the border, using fusible web appliqué method. Sew buttonhole stitch around the appliqué edges.

JEWEL TONE QUILT
INNER BORDER

1. Measure, cut and sew two of the 1½"-wide dark strips to the top and bottom of the quilt.

2. Repeat for the sides of the quilt, using remaining strips to piece borders for needed length.

MIDDLE BORDER

1. Repeat Step 1 for Inner Border, using the 1¼"-wide pink dot strips.

2. Repeat Step 2 for Inner Border.

OUTER BORDER

1. Repeat Step 1 for Inner Border, using the 5½"-wide dark strips.

2. Repeat Step 2 for Inner Border.

COUNTRY SUNFLOWERS PLACE MATS

Place mats are a quick and easy way to display the fabulous log cabin style.

Finished Place Mat: 14" x 19"   Finished Block: 7"

Fabric	Cut	For
Red	16 squares, 1½" x 1½"	Centers
Red	8 strips, 2¼" wide	Binding
Tan	16 squares, 1½" x 1½"	Log 1
Tan	16 rectangles, 1½" x 2½"	Log 2
Tan	4 flower centers using template C	Flower centers
Turquoise blue	16 rectangles, 1½" x 2½"	Log 3
Turquoise blue	16 rectangles, 1½" x 3½"	Log 4
Gold	16 rectangles, 1½" x 3½"	Log 5
Gold	16 rectangles, 1½" x 4½"	Log 6
Medium blue	16 rectangles, 1½" x 4½"	Log 7
Medium blue	16 rectangles, 1½" x 5½"	Log 8
Medium brown	16 rectangles, 1½" x 5½"	Log 9
Medium brown	16 rectangles, 1½" x 6½"	Log 10
Medium dark blue	16 rectangles, 1½" x 6½"	Log 11
Medium dark blue	16 rectangles, 1½" x 7½"	Log 12
Dark brown	8 rectangles, 3" x 14½"	Side borders
Dark brown	4 large flower centers using Template B	Large sunflower centers
Dark green	4 stems using Template E	Stems
Golden yellow	4 flower petals using Template A	Sunflower petals
Light green	8 leaves using Template D	Sunflower leaves
Backing	4 rectangles, 16" x 21"	
Batting	4 rectangles, 16" x 21"	

Materials (Makes 4)

⅝ yd. red fabric
¼ yd. tan fabric
¼ yd. turquoise blue fabric
¼ yd. gold fabric
¼ yd. medium blue fabric
¼ yd. medium brown fabric
⅜ yd. medium dark blue fabric
½ yd. dark brown fabric
⅛ yd. dark green fabric
¼ yd. golden yellow fabric
⅛ yd. light green fabric
1 yd. backing
⅝ yd. fusible web
1 yd. batting (45" wide)
Sewing tools and supplies

NOTE: *Before cutting appliqué pieces, refer to Fusible Web Appliqué section in How-to Quilting Basics.*

Block Construction

Construct the log cabin blocks as directed for the Country Sunflowers Quilt. There will be 12 logs (three rounds) instead of 16 logs (four rounds). For vines, use Template E or bias strips and bias bar (see Country Sunflowers Quilt instructions or page 27).

Place Mat Assembly

1. Sew four blocks together in a Sunshine and Shadows pattern as illustrated.

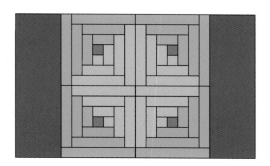

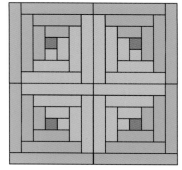

Center Place Mat

2. Sew a 3" x 14½" rectangle to opposite sides of the place mat center.

3. Using the fusible web appliqué method, cut out and appliqué the sunflower vine and stem to each of the place mats using Templates A Small, B Small, C Small, D Small, and E. Sew buttonhole stitch around appliqué edges.

Finishing

1. Layer and quilt. Place mats are quilted in a crosshatch pattern (parallel diagonal lines that intersect) using a 2" grid.

2. Trim off extra batting and bind.

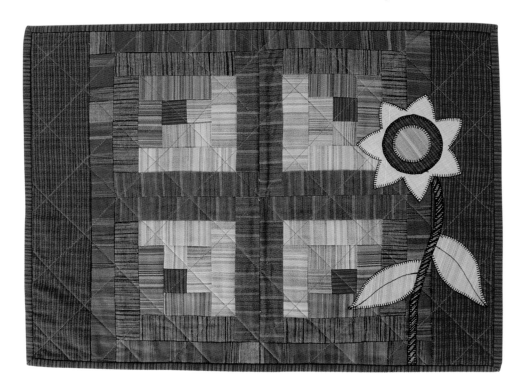

Finished Tote Bag: 18½" x 20¾"   Finished Block: 9"

JEWEL TOTE BAG

Form and function unite in this stylish tote. It's a great project that can be completed in no time.

Fabric	Cut	For
Bright pink	8 squares, 1½" x 1½"	Centers
Bright pink	2 rectangles, 3¼" x 18½"	Top edge
Pink, green, purple print	8 squares, 1½" x 1½"	Log 1
Pink, green, purple print	8 rectangles, 1½" x 2½"	Log 2
Purple	8 rectangles, 1½" x 3½"	Log 5
Purple	8 rectangles, 1½" x 4½"	Log 6
Purple and teal	8 rectangles, 1½" x 5½"	Log 9
Purple and teal	8 rectangles, 1½" x 6½"	Log 10
Teal	8 rectangles, 1½" x 7½"	Log 13
Teal	8 rectangles, 1½" x 8½"	Log 14
Black	8 rectangles, 1½" x 2½"	Log 3
Black	8 rectangles, 1½" x 3½"	Log 4
Black	8 rectangles, 1½" x 4½"	Log 7
Black	8 rectangles, 1½" x 5½"	Log 8
Black	8 rectangles, 1½" x 6½"	Log 11
Black	8 rectangles, 1½" x 7½"	Log 12
Black	8 rectangles, 1½" x 8½"	Log 15
Black	8 rectangles, 1½" x 9½"	Log 16
Black	2 rectangles, 4" x 29"	Handles
Black	2 rectangles, 21¼" x 18½" (measure bag; adjust to fit)	Lining
Batting	2 rectangles, 24" x 21" (measure bag; adjust to fit)	Bag
Batting	2 strips, 1½" x 28"	Handles

Materials

¼ yd. bright pink fabric
⅛ yd. pink, green, purple multi-color print fabric
⅛ yd. purple fabric
¼ yd. purple and teal fabric
¼ yd. teal fabric
1½ yd. black fabric
⅞ yd. batting (44" wide)
3⅛ yd. backing
Sewing tools and supplies

Block Construction

Construct the blocks as directed for the Country Sunflowers Quilt.

Make 2

Tote Bag Assembly

1. Sew four blocks together in the Sunshine and Shadows pattern as illustrated. Make 2 (one front and one back).

2. Sew a 3¼" x 18½" bright pink dot strip to the top front and top back of the tote bag.

Make 2

3. Lay the bag front, right side up, on batting and baste together. Quilt bag to batting. Repeat for back. Trim extra batting.

4. Lay the lining on the bag front, right sides together, and sew across the top edge.

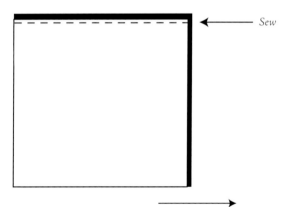

← *Sew*

5. Open and press the seam toward the quilted portion of the bag.

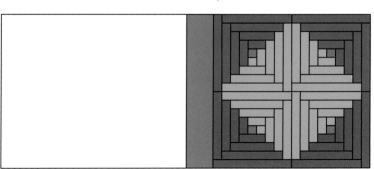

Bag/Lining Unit

6. Lay the two bag/lining units, right sides together, and stitch around the entire unit, leaving a 4" opening for turning.

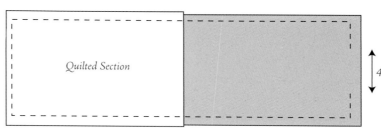

7. Turn the bag right side out through the opening and sew opening closed. Tuck the lining to the inside of the bag. Stitch close to the top edge of the bag to hold the lining in place.

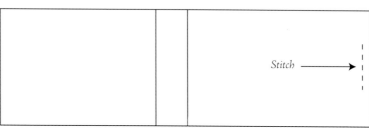

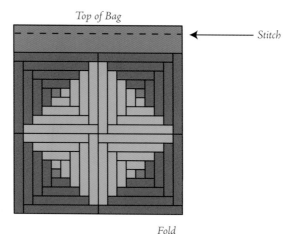

8. Fold under ½", wrong sides together, on both edges of the 4" x 29" strip. Repeat for the second strip.

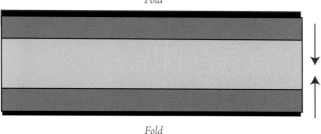

9. Fold one 29" strip in half lengthwise, wrong sides together, and press. Repeat for the second strip.

10. Open the strip and on the wrong side of the fabric, lay a 1½" x 28" strip of batting against the center fold of the strip, leaving ½" from each end free of batting. Place the ½" fold over the top of the batting. Repeat for the second strip.

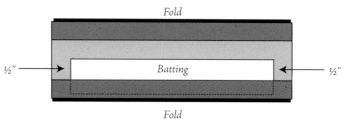

11. Fold the handles in half lengthwise, lining up the two ½" folded edges. Sandwich the batting between the top and bottom of the handle. Pin to secure and sew ⅛" from the edge as illustrated.

½" Folded Edges

12. Fold the two raw-edge ends under ½" and press.

½" ½"

3½"

13. Measure 3½" from both edges of the bag and mark with chalk or marker.

14. Place the outside edge of the handle against the marked lines with the bottom of the strip against the border seam. Sew in place as illustrated. Repeat for reverse side of the bag.

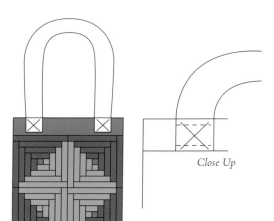

Close Up

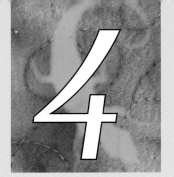

4

NINE-PATCH

The simple nine-patch pattern is one of the easiest blocks to construct, and it is a favorite of both beginners and experienced quilters alike. This block endures because of its versatility and design possibilities.

STARS AND SQUARES QUILT

To add interest, I designed this nine-patch using two colors (blue and pink) that weave throughout the quilt. It also uses a fun, colorful border you'll love.

Finished Quilt: 38" x 38"   Finished Block: 6"

Materials

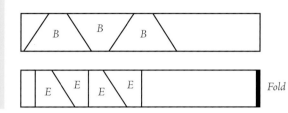

15⁄8 yd. yellow fabric
½ yd. blue fabric
½ yd. pink fabric
5⁄6 yd. green fabric
½ yd. fusible web
1¼ yd. backing
1¼ yd. batting
Sewing tools and supplies

Fabric	Cut	For
Yellow	3 strips, 3½" wide. Cut into 64 triangles using Template B (*see illustration above*)	Pieced outer border
Yellow	1 strip, 3½" wide. With the strip folded in half, wrong sides together, cut 4 triangles and 4 reverse triangles using template E. (*see illustration above*)	Border corner unit
Yellow	Cut the remainder of the strip to 2⅜", then cut 2 squares, 2⅜" x 2⅜". Cut each square once on the diagonal for a total of 4 triangles using Template F	Border corner unit
Yellow	6 strips, 2½" wide	Strip sets
Yellow	2 strips. Cut into 12 squares, 6½" x 6½"	Background
Yellow	4 strips, 2¼"	Binding
Blue	Cut 2 strips, 3½" wide. Cut into 28 triangles using Template B (*see illustration above*)	Pieced outer border
Blue	Fold the remainder of the strip in half, wrong sides together, cut 4 triangles and 4 reverse triangles using Template C Each cut will make one C and one C reverse	Corner triangles
Blue	Cut 3 strips, 2½" wide	Strip sets
Pink	2 strips, 3⅝" wide. Cut into 32 triangles using Template B (*see illustration above*)	Pieced outer border
Pink	3 strips, 2½" wide	Strip sets
Green	1 strip, 3¾" wide. Cut into 4 triangles using Template D	Corner triangle D
Green	4 strips, 1½" wide	Inner border
Green	Use remaining fabric to cut 12 stars using Template A	Stars

NOTE: *Before cutting appliqué pieces, refer to Fusible Web Appliqué section in How-to Quilting Basics.*

Block Construction

BLOCKS A AND B – NINE-PATCH BLOCKS

1. Sew 2½" strips of blue, yellow, and pink together to make Groups 1 - 3 as illustrated. Cut into 2½"-wide segments. Press toward the arrows.

2½"

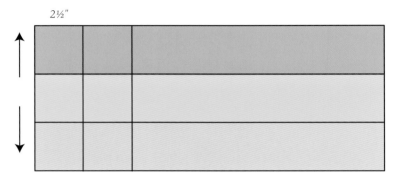

Group 1
Make 2 Strip Sets
Cut into 26 Segments

2½"

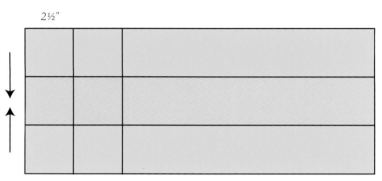

Group 2
Make 1 Strip Set,
Cut into 9 Segments

2½"

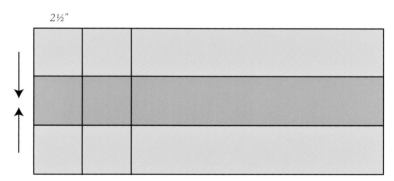

Group 3
Make 1 Strip Set
Cut into 4 Segments

2. Sew two Group 1 segments together with one Group 2 segment as illustrated to make Block A.

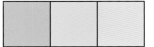

+

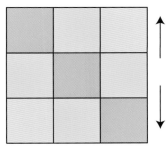

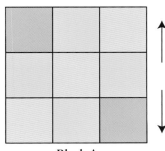

Block A
Make 9

3. Sew two Group 1 segments together with one Group 3 segment as illustrated to make Block B.

Block B
Make 4

BLOCK C – APPLIQUÉ STAR BLOCK

Using the fusible web appliqué method, center a green star on a 6½" yellow square and sew around star edges using the buttonhole stitch.

Quilt Assembly

Arrange the quilt pieces as illustrated, with 5 rows of 5 blocks each. Sew blocks to complete rows first; press toward the star blocks. Sew rows together; press seams away from center row.

Borders

NOTE: *Refer to Borders section in How-to Quilting Basics for detailed border instructions.*

INNER BORDER

1. Measure, cut and sew two of the 1½"-wide green strips to the top and bottom of the quilt.
2. Repeat for the sides of the quilt.

OUTER BORDER

1. Sew a yellow Template E piece to both sides of a green Template D piece to make Unit 1. Make 4.
2. Sew a 2⅜" yellow triangle (F) to a Unit 1 to complete the Corner Unit. Make 4.
3. Use Template B in alternating colors to make the side border, starting and ending with a blue Template C triangle. Sew border units as shown in the photo. Press seams open. Make 4.

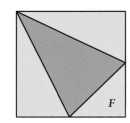

Unit 1
Make 4

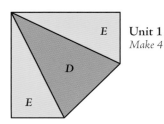

Corner Unit
Make 4

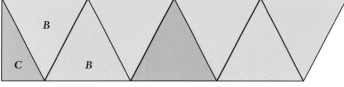

Make 4

4. Sew a pieced border unit to the top and bottom of the quilt.
5. Sew corner units to each end of side borders and sew to the sides of the quilt.

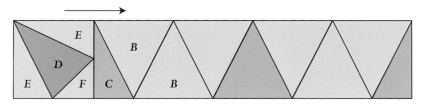 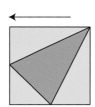

> **TIP** If the border unit is too long or too short, adjust seam allowances slightly in equal increments across the border unit until length is correct.

Finishing

Layer, quilt and bind. Refer to Finishing section in How-to Quilting Basics for detailed instructions.

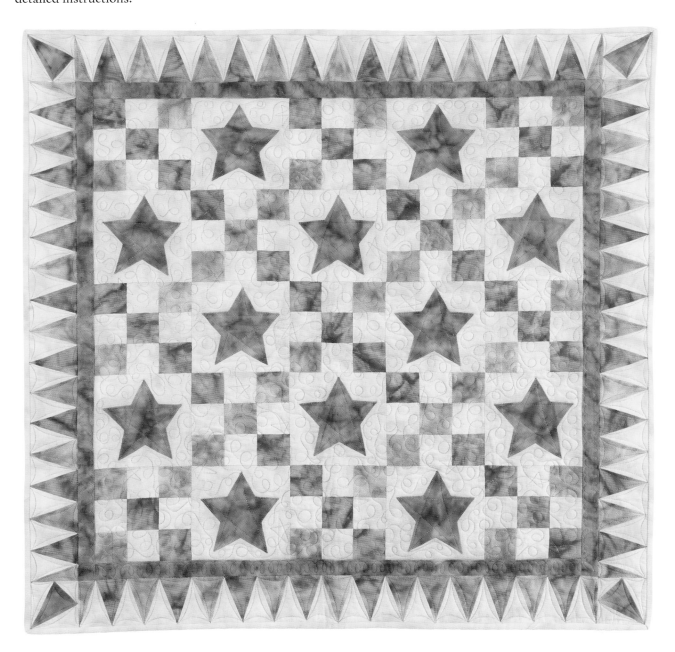

Finished Quilt: 54½" x 81½"   Finished Block: 13½"

SUNNY-SIDE UP QUILT

This double nine-patch quilt makes use of a novelty print as a focal point. The coordinating fabrics were selected to carry out the country kitchen theme. To provide added interest, I selected a double-nine patch layout using strong contrasting colors to weave throughout the quilt.

Materials

1¾ yd. novelty fabric
   (approx. yardage)
1¼ yd. small cream floral print fabric
⅞ yd. small black floral print fabric
⅝ yd. red print fabric
⅜ yd. solid black fabric
1¼ yd. large black floral print fabric
3½ yd. backing
61" x 88" batting
Sewing tools and supplies

TIP Select the novelty print and then find coordinating fabrics. Use a variety of scales and textures to add dimension to your quilt.

Fabric	Cut	For
Novelty	7 squares, 14" x 14", using a template or large grid ruler	Plain squares
Novelty	4 squares, 5" x 5", using a template or large grid ruler	Corners
Small cream floral	4 strips. Cut into 32 squares, 5" x 5"	Alternating squares
Small cream floral	10 strips, 2" wide	Strip sets
Small black floral	6 strips, 2" wide	Strip sets
Small black floral	7 strips, 2¼" wide	Binding
Red print	5 strips, 2" wide	Strip sets
Red print	5 strips, 2" wide	Middle border
Solid black	6 strips, 1¾" wide	Inner border
Large black floral	7 strips, 5½" wide	Outer border

Block Construction

BLOCKS A AND B – DOUBLE NINE-PATCH BLOCKS

1. Sew 2" strips of small black floral, cream floral and red print together to make Groups 1 - 3 as shown. Cut the groups into 2"-wide segments. Press toward arrows.

Group 1
Make 4 Strip Sets, Cut into 80 Segments

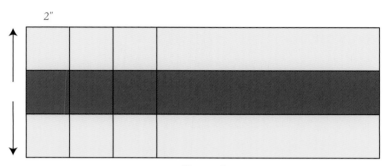

Group 2
Make 2 Strip Sets, Cut into 26 Segments

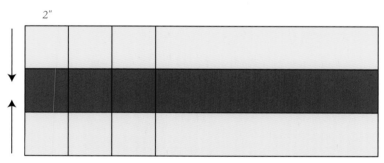

Group 3
Make 1 Strip Set, Cut into 14 Segments

2. Sew Group 1 segments and Group 2 segments together to make Unit 1.

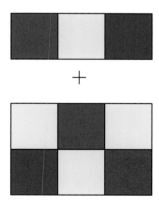

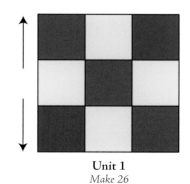

Unit 1
Make 26

3. Sew Group 1 segments and Group 3 segments together to make Unit 2.

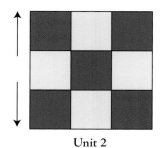

Unit 2
Make 14

4. Sew a Unit 1 to opposite sides of a 5" square of small cream floral.

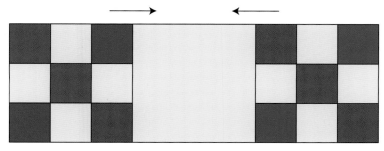

Section 1
Make 12

5. Sew a Unit 2 to opposite sides of a 5" square of small cream floral.

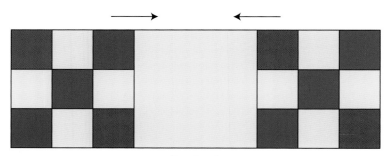

Section 2
Make 4

6. Sew a 5" square of small cream floral to opposite sides of a Unit 2.

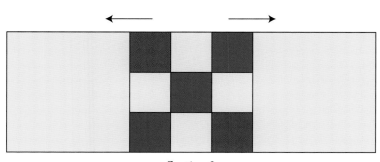

Section 3
Make 6

7. Sew a 5" square of small cream floral to opposite sides of a Unit 1.

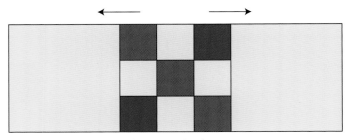

Section 4, Make 2

8. Sew a Section 1 to the top and bottom of a Section 3 to make Block A.

Block A, Make 6

9. Sew a Section 2 to the top and bottom of a Section 4 to make Block B.

Block B, Make 2

Quilt Assembly

1. Sew one Block A to opposite side of a 14" square of novelty print.

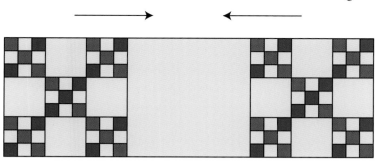

Make 3 Rows

2. Sew a 14" square of novelty print to opposite sides of one Block B.

Make 2 Rows

3. Arrange the quilt pieces as illustrated with 5 rows of 3 blocks each. Sew rows together; press seams away from the center row.

A	Novelty	A
Novelty	B	Novelty
A	Novelty	A
Novelty	B	Novelty
A	Novelty	A

Rows 1-5 completed

Borders

NOTE: *Refer to Borders section in How-to Quilting Basics for detailed border instructions.*

INNER BORDER

1. Measure, cut and sew two of the 1¾"-wide black strips to the top and bottom of the quilt.
2. Repeat for the sides of the quilt, using remaining strips to piece borders for needed length.

MIDDLE BORDER

1. Repeat Step 1 of Inner Border, using the 1¼"-wide red print strips.
2. Repeat Step 2 of Inner Border.

OUTER BORDER

1. Measure and cut the 5½"-wide large black floral strips for the top and bottom. Do not sew to the quilt.
2. Measure and cut the remaining 5½"-wide strips for the sides of the quilt.
3. Sew a 5½" square corner unit to each end of the side borders.
4. Sew borders to the top and bottom of the quilt, and then sew the side borders to the quilt.

Finishing

Layer, quilt and bind. Refer to Finishing
section in How-to Quilting Basics for
detailed instructions.

Finished Pillow: 17" x 17"

Sunny-Side Up Pillow

A fast and fun-to-make pillow is just the thing for a cozy, coordinated room.

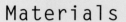

Materials

½ yd. novelty fabric
⅞ yd. small cream floral print fabric
⅛ yd. small black floral print fabric
¼ yd. red print fabric
⅜ yd. solid black fabric
1¼ yd. large black floral print fabric
2½ yd. cording ($^3/_{16}$")
20" x 20" batting (low-loft polyester
    or cotton)
18" x 18" pillow form
Sewing tools and supplies

Fabric	Cut	For
Novelty	1 square, 9½" x 9½", using a template or large grid ruler	Plain square
Small cream floral	2 strips, 2" wide	Strip sets
Small cream floral	1 strip. Cut into 4 squares, 3½" x 3½"	Corner units
Small cream floral	2 strips, 1¾" wide. Cut into 2 rectangles, 1¾" x 15½"	Top and bottom borders
Small cream floral	Remaining strip into 2 rectangles, 1¾" x 18"	Side borders
Small cream floral	1 square, 18" x 18"	Pillow back
Small black floral	1 strip, 2" wide	Strip sets
Red print	1 strip, 2" wide	Strip sets
Red print	2 strips, 1" wide	Cording strip
Red print	4 heart appliqués	Hearts

NOTE: *Before cutting appliqué pieces, refer to Fusible Web Appliqué section in How-to Quilting Basics.*

Pillow Front Block Construction

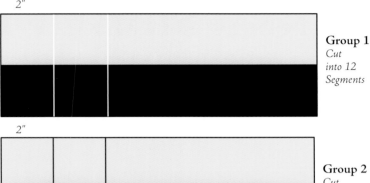

Group 1
Cut into 12 Segments

Group 2
Cut into 12 Segments

1. Sew 2"-wide strips of small black floral and cream floral together as illustrated to make Group 1. Sew 2"-wide strips of red print and cream floral together as illustrated to make Group 2. Cut the groups into 2"-wide segments.

2. Sew segments together as illustrated to form patchwork border units.

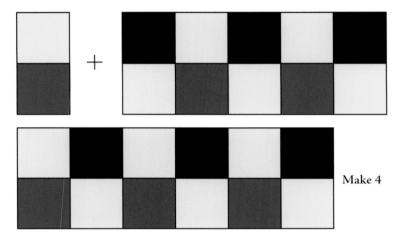

Make 4

3. Sew a border unit to the top and bottom of the 9½" pillow center.

4. Using the fusible web appliqué method, center hearts to the 3½" corner squares and appliqué using the buttonhole stitch.

5. Sew a heart corner unit to the top and bottom of two patchwork border units. Sew to the sides of the pillow center.

6. Sew a 1¾" x 15½" cream strip to the top and bottom of the pillow. Sew a 1¾" x 18½" strip to each side of the pillow.

7. Place the pieced pillow, right side up, on top of the batting. Baste and quilt.

Left Side Border

Right Side Border

Pillow Assembly/Finishing

CORDING

1. Place the two strips of 1"-wide red print cording fabric, right sides together, with ends at right angles. Draw a line from A to B as illustrated. Sew on marked line and trim ¼" from the sewn line. Press seam open.

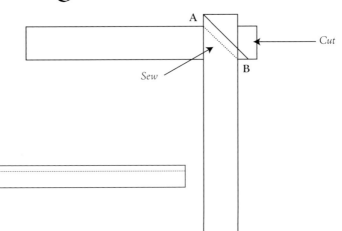

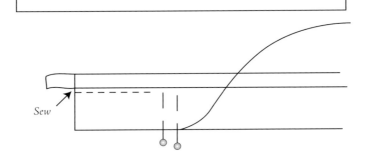

2. Insert a zipper foot on the sewing machine, with the needle on the right side of the foot. Center the cording on the wrong side of the cording strip. Matching the raw edges, fold the cording strip over the cording. Pin and sew next to the cording.

3. Pin the cording around the pillow front, starting at the bottom center of the pillow front, leaving a 2" tail. Clip the piping seam allowance at each corner so the piping will lay flat at the corners. Using the zipper foot, sew piping to the pillow. Sew next to the cording (the seam allowance will be ½"). Overlap the ends and stitch. Trim cording even with seam allowance. Trim corners.

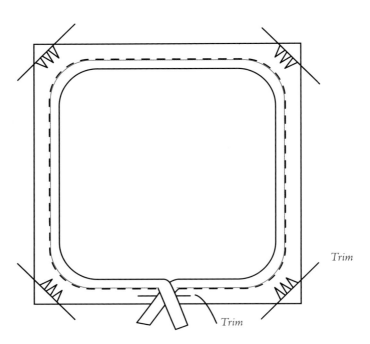

4. Lay the pillow front on top of an 18"
   square of pillow backing, right sides
   facing, and pin together. Using a zipper
   foot, sew on top of the previous stitching (from sewing the piping to the pillow), leaving a 14" to 15" opening at the
   bottom center for inserting the pillow
   form.

5. Turn the pillow right side out, and
   insert the 18" pillow form.

6. Turn under the seam allowance of the
   open edge on the back of the pillow. Pin
   opening and stitch closed.

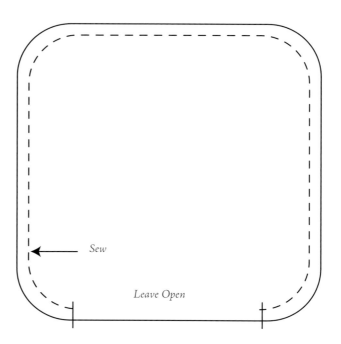

Sew

Leave Open

5

WIND IN THE PINES

Based on two traditional blocks, the unique patterns in this chapter are sure to look and feel familiar, and they provide a fresh appeal to quilters of all skill levels.

Block Basics

The block used for the quilts and projects in this chapter is based on two traditional blocks, the Pine Tree block and the Pinwheel block. Combining blocks to make a new block brings interesting and unique design elements to the projects. The quilt has the look and feel of an on-point setting of the blocks, but is pieced like a straight setting. In designing a combined block, both of the blocks must be the same size. One of the blocks must be able to be quartered and pieced in quarter sections. Each quarter section is then sewn to the sides of the second block.

The quilts and projects in this chapter have the same size block, but with a totally different fabric selection.

The small quilt, or in this case a table-cloth, has bright colors and lots of color contrast. The use and placement of the dots, large and small prints, and plaids provides a textural difference that creates motion.

The lap quilt has less color contrast and uses a softer color palette. This quilt uses the scale or size difference of various prints to create the interest.

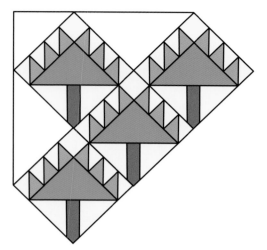

On-Point Setting

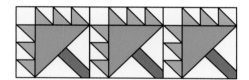

Straight Setting

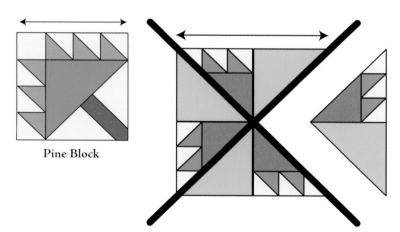

Pine Block

**Pinwheel Block, Pinwheel Block
Quarter Section, sew to Pine Block**

WIND IN THE PINES PLACE MATS

Serve up a cup of tea on these colorful place mats. For the best results, choose a large-print fabric for the border.

Finished Size: 19¾" x 12¾"   Finished Block: 12¾"

Materials (Makes 4)

⅛ yd. brown print fabric
¼ yd. dark blue print fabric
⅜ yd. large red print fabric
¾ yd. red plaid print fabric
⅜ yd. yellow fabric
¼ yd. green print fabric
⅝ yd. cream with red print fabric
⅛ yd. red solid fabric
⅜ yd. large blue print fabric
1 yd. backing (your choice)
1 yd. batting (45" wide cotton or
  heat-resistant lining)
Sewing tools and supplies

Fabric	Cut	For
Brown print	1 strip, 1¾" wide. Cut into 4 tree trunks using Template A *(see illustration above)*	Tree trunks
Dark blue print	2 strips. Cut into 16 squares, 2⅝" x 2⅝"	Pinwheel points
Large red print	1 strip. Cut into 2 squares, 7⅝" x 7⅝", cut each square across the diagonal	Tree top
Red plaid print	1 strip. Cut into 4 squares, 5½" x 5½", cut each square across both diagonals	Small pinwheel triangles
Red plaid print	8 strips, 2¼" wide	Binding
Yellow floral	1 strip. Cut into 4 squares, 7⅝" x 7⅝", cut each square across both diagonals	Large pinwheel triangles
Green print	1 strip. Cut into 12 squares, 3⅜" x 3⅜"	Tree points
Cream with red print	1 strip. Cut into 12 squares, 3⅜" x 3⅜"	Tree points
Cream with red print	1 strip. Cut into 4 squares, 2¾" x 2¾"	Background squares
Cream with red print	2 strips. Cut into 16 squares, 2⅝" x 2⅝"	Pinwheel points
Cream with red print	1 strip. Cut into 8 squares, 2⅜" x 2⅜", cut each square once across the diagonal	Background triangles
Cream with red print	9 squares, 5" x 5", cut once across the diagonal	Tree trunk background
Red solid	3 strips, 1" wide	Inner border
Large blue print	3 strips, 3¼" wide. Cut into 8 rectangles, 3¼" x 12¾"	Outer border
Backing	2 strips, 16" wide. Cut into 4 rectangles, 16" x 21"	
Batting	4 rectangles, 16" x 21"	

Wind in the Pines Place Mat Construction

PINWHEEL UNIT CONSTRUCTION

NOTE: *Refer to Pinwheel Unit Construction for Tablecloth for additional illustrations.*

1. Draw a diagonal line across the wrong side of 16 of the 2⅝" background squares. Place right sides together with 16 of the 2⅝" squares of blue print. Sew ¼" on each side of the diagonal line. Cut on the solid line across the diagonal. Open squares and press. Make 32.
2. Place a 2" template on top of each of the squares with the diagonal template line centered on the diagonal seam. Trim squares to 2".
3. Arrange the Pinwheel Unit and sew together.

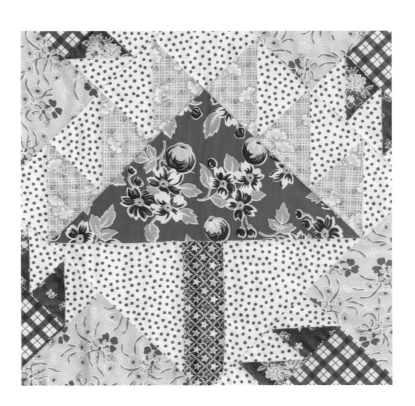

PINE TREE CENTER BLOCK CONSTRUCTION

NOTE: *Refer to Pinwheel Unit Construction for Tablecloth for additional illustrations.*

1. Draw a diagonal line across the wrong side of 12 of the 3⅜" background squares. Place right sides together with 12 of the 3⅜" green squares. Sew ¼" on each side of the diagonal line. Cut on the solid line across the diagonal. Open squares and press seams open. Make 24.
2. Place a 2¾" square template on top of each of the squares with the diagonal template line centered on the diagonal seam. Trim squares to 2¾".
3. Arrange the Pine Tree Block and sew together.
4. Sew the Pinwheel Units to the Pine Tree Blocks. Make 4.

Borders

1. For inner side border, sew a 1½" x 12¾" red solid strip to opposite sides of the Wind in the Pines Block.

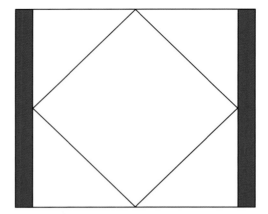

2. For outer side border, sew a 3¼" x 12¾" large blue print strip to the sides of each 1½" red solid.

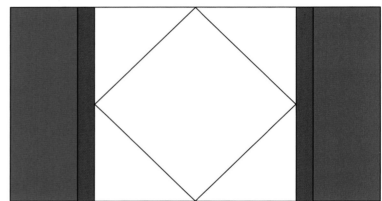

Finishing

Layer, quilt, and bind. Refer to Finishing section in How-to Quilting Basics for detailed instructions.

WIND IN THE PINES TABLECLOTH

Combining on-point and straight settings is a wonderful technique that results in squares the whole family will love.

Finished Size: 51¾" x 51¾"   Finished Block: 12¾" (with pieced corners added)

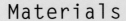

Materials

¼ yd. brown print fabric
⅜ yd. dark blue print fabric
⅜ yd. large red print fabric
¾ yd. red plaid print fabric
⅝ yd. yellow floral fabric
⅜ yd. green print fabric
1⅛ yd. cream with red print fabric
¼ yd. solid red fabric
1 yd. large blue print fabric
3¼ yd. backing
58" x 58" batting
Sewing tools and supplies

Fabric	Cut	For
Brown print	2 strips, 1¾" wide. Cut into 9 tree trunks using Template A *(see illustration above)*	Tree trunks
Dark blue print	3 strips. Cut into 36 squares, 2⅝" x 2⅝"	Pinwheel points
Large red print	1 strip. Cut into 5 squares, 7⅝" x 7⅝". Cut each square across the diagonal for 10 triangles	Tree tops
Red plaid print	2 strips. Cut into 9 squares, 5½" x 5½". Cut each square across both diagonals	Small pinwheel triangles
Red plaid print	5 strips, 2¼" wide	Binding
Yellow floral	2 strips. Cut into 9 squares, 7⅝" x 7⅝". Cut each square across both diagonals	Large pinwheel triangles
Green print	3 strips. Cut into 27 squares, 3⅜" x 3⅜". Cut each square across the diagonal	Tree points
Cream with red print	3 strips. Cut into 27 squares, 3⅜" x 3⅜". Cut once across the diagonal	Tree points
Cream with red print	1 strip. Cut into 9 squares, 2¾" x 2¾"	Background
Cream with red print	3 strips. Cut into 36 squares, 2⅝" x 2⅝"	Pinwheel points
Cream with red print	2 strips. Cut into 18 squares, 2⅜" x 2⅜". Cut once across the diagonal	Background triangles for pinwheels
Cream with red print	2 strips. Cut into 9 squares, 5" x 5". Cut once across the diagonal	Tree trunk background
Red solid	4 strips, 1½" wide	Inner border
Large blue print	5 strips, 6" wide	Outer border

Construction instructions to follow on page 77.

NOTE: *Before cutting, refer to Hint for Perfect Narrow Borders in How-to Quilting Basics.*

WIND IN THE PINES LAP QUILT

Fall in love with the delicate colors featured in this powerful design.

Finished Size: 50¼" x 63"   Finished Block: 12¾" (with pieced corner units added)

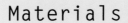

Materials

¼ yd. warm brown print fabric
⅜ yd. dark pink print fabric
1¾ yd. large pink print fabric
¾ yd. light orange fabric
⅝ yd. dark green fabric
1¼ yd. cream with green print fabric
½ yd. pink stripe fabric (binding)
3¼ yd. backing
56" x 69" batting
Sewing tools and supplies

Fabric	Cut	For
Warm brown print	Cut 2 strips, 1¾" wide. Cut into 12 tree trunks using Template A. *(see illustration above)*	Tree trunks
Dark pink print	4 strips. Cut into 48 squares, 2⅝" x 2⅝"	Pinwheel points
Large pink print	2 strips. Cut into 6 squares, 7⅝" x 7⅝". Cut each square across diagonal	Tree tops
Large pink print	2 strips. Cut into 12 squares, 5½" x 5½". Cut each square across diagonal	Small pinwheel triangles
Large pink print	5 strips, 5½" wide	Outer border
Light orange	3 strips. Cut into 12 squares, 7⅝" x 7⅝". Cut each square across diagonal	Large pinwheel triangles
Dark green	3 strips. Cut into 36 squares, 3⅜" x 3⅜"	Tree points
Dark green	5 strips, 1½" wide	Inner border
Cream with green print	3 strips. Cut into 36 squares, 3⅜" x 3⅜". Cut each square across diagonal	Tree points
Cream with green print	1 strip. Cut into 12 squares, 2¾" x 2¾"	Background squares
Cream with green print	4 strips. Cut into 48 squares, 2⅝" x 2⅝"	Pinwheel points
Cream with green print	2 strips. Cut into 24 squares, 2⅜" x 2⅜". Cut each square across diagonal	Background triangles
Cream with green print	2 strips. Cut into 12 squares, 5" x 5". Cut each square across diagonal	Tree trunk background
Pink stripe	Cut 6 strips, 2¼" wide	Binding

NOTE: *Before cutting, refer to Hint for Perfect Narrow Borders in How-to Quilting Basics.*

Block Construction

NOTE: *Piecing instructions are for both tablecloth and quilt sizes. Text and numbers for the Wind in the Pines Lap Quilt are in parenthesis.*

PINWHEEL UNITS CONSTRUCTION

1. Draw a diagonal line across the wrong side of 36 (48) of the 2⅝" background squares. Place right sides together with 36 (48) of the 2⅝" blue print (dark pink print) squares. Sew ¼" on each side of the diagonal line. Cut on the solid line across the diagonal. Open squares and press seams open. Make 72 (96).

2. Place a 2" square template on top of each of the squares with the diagonal template line centered on the diagonal seam. Trim squares to 2" as illustrated .

3. Arrange the Pinwheel Unit and sew together as illustrated below.

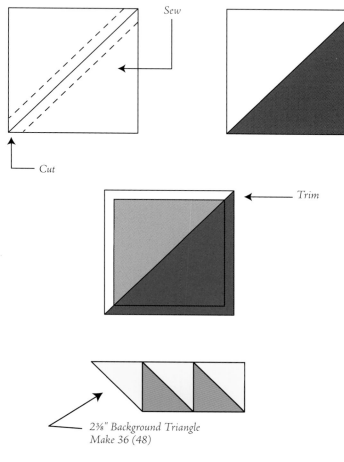

Sew

Cut

Trim

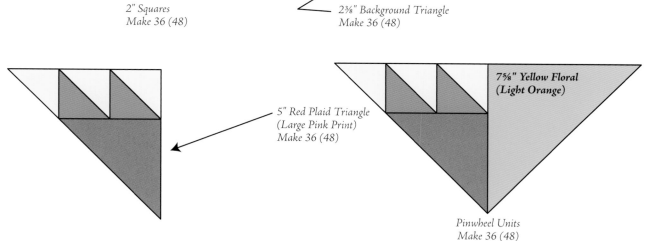

2" Squares
Make 36 (48)

2⅜" Background Triangle
Make 36 (48)

5" Red Plaid Triangle
(Large Pink Print)
Make 36 (48)

7⅝" Yellow Floral
(Light Orange)

Pinwheel Units
Make 36 (48)

PINE TREE CENTER BLOCK CONSTRUCTION

1. Draw a diagonal line across the wrong side of 27 (36) of the 3⅜" background squares. Place right sides together with 27 (36) of the 3⅜" green (dark green) squares. Sew ¼" on each side of the diagonal line. Cut on the solid line across the diagonal. Open squares and press seams open. Make 54 (72). See illustration for constructing the Pinwheel Unit.

2. Place a 2¾" square template on top of each of the squares with the diagonal template line centered on the diagonal seam. Trim squares to 2¾".

3. Arrange the Pine Tree Block and sew together as illustrated.

4. Sew the Tree Top Unit to the Tree Trunk Unit.

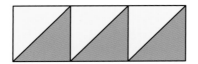

2¾" Squares
Make 9 (12) Tree Top Units

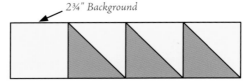

2¾" Background

Make 9 (12)

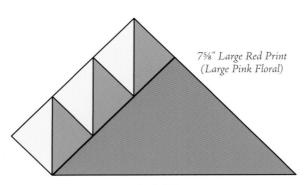

7⅝" Large Red Print
(Large Pink Floral)

Make 9 (12)

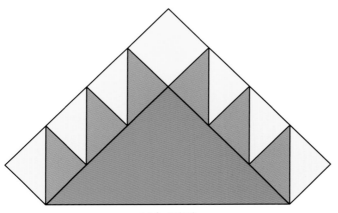

Make 9 (12)
Treetop Units

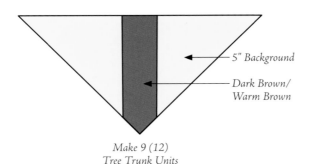

5" Background

Dark Brown/
Warm Brown

Make 9 (12)
Tree Trunk Units

Pine Tree Block
Make 9 (12)

WIND IN THE PINES BLOCK CONSTRUCTION

1. Sew a Pinwheel Unit to two opposite sides of a Pine Tree Block.

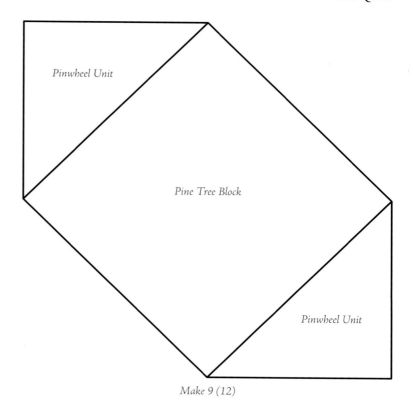

Pinwheel Unit

Pine Tree Block

Pinwheel Unit

Make 9 (12)

2. Sew a Pinwheel Unit to the two remaining sides of the Pine Tree Block.

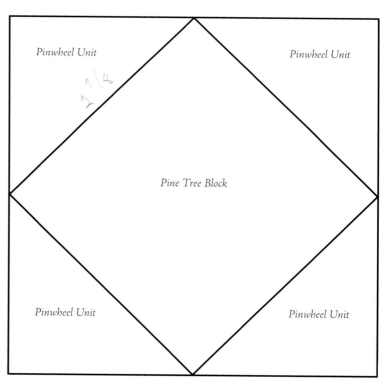

Pinwheel Unit

Pinwheel Unit

Pine Tree Block

Pinwheel Unit

Pinwheel Unit

Completed Block
Make 9 (12)

Quilt Assembly

1. Arrange the tablecloth pieces in 3 rows of 3 blocks each. Sew rows together; press seams away from the center row
2. Arrange the lap quilt pieces in 3 rows of 4 blocks each. Sew rows together; press seams away from the center row.

Borders

Note: *Refer to Borders section in How-to Quilting Basics for detailed border instructions.*

TABLECLOTH INNER BORDER

Note: *See the Hint for Perfect Narrow Borders in How-to Quilting Basics.*

1. Measure, cut and sew two of the 1½"-wide red strips to the top and bottom of the quilt.
2. Repeat for the sides of the quilt.

TABLECLOTH OUTER BORDER

1. Repeat Step 1 for Inner Border, using the 6"-wide large blue print strips.
2. Repeat for the sides of the quilt, using three strips to piece borders for needed length.

LAP QUILT INNER BORDER

1. Measure, cut and sew two of the 1½"-wide dark green strips to the top and bottom of the quilt.
2. Repeat for the sides of the quilt, using three strips to piece borders for needed length.

LAP QUILT OUTER BORDER

1. Repeat Step 1 for Inner Border, using the 5½"-wide large pink print strips.
2. Repeat for the sides of the quilt, using three strips to piece borders for needed length.

Finishing

Layer, quilt and bind. Refer to Finishing
section in How-to Quilting Basics for
detailed instructions.

Finished Tablecloth

Finished Lap Quilt

WIND IN THE PINES NAPKINS

Here's a quick project that will be a big hit the next time you entertain guests for dinner! Perfect for using up scraps from your stash.

Finished Size: 16" x 16"

Materials
(Makes 4)

1⅛ yd. large red print fabric
Sewing tools and supplies

Fabric	Cut	For
Large red print	2 strips. Cut into 4 squares, 17" x 17"	Napkin square

Napkin Finishing

1. Turn the edges of the napkins under ¼" and press. Turn each side under another ¼" and press.
2. Stitch close to the edge, or if a serger machine is available, serge around the edges.

6

DRUNKARD'S PATH

The Drunkard's Path, also known as the Fool's Puzzle, is easy to piece since there are only two pieces used to construct the block. The trick, however, lies in piecing the curves. It's the wide variety of layout possibilities that make it so exciting.

Finished Pillow: 16½" x 16½"

DRUNKARD'S PATH PILLOW

This pillow uses the most common of the drunkard path layouts. It creates a unique design that adds real excitement to a room.

Materials

⅜ yd. white fabric
¾ yd. green print fabric
¼ yd. yellow print fabric
⅛ yd. golden yellow solid fabric
18" x 18" pillow form
2½ yd. cording (³⁄₁₆")
Sewing tools and supplies

Fabric	Cut	For
White	1 strip, 3⅜" wide. Cut into 8 paths using Template A	Paths
White	1 strip, 4" wide. Cut into 8 paths using Template B	Background
White	2 strips, 2" wide	Outer border
Green print	1 strip, 4" wide. Cut into 4 paths using Template B	Paths
Green print	Cut the strip to measure 3⅜" wide. Cut into 4 paths using Template A	Paths
Green print	2 strips, 1" wide	Cording
Green print	1 square, 17½" x 17½"	Pillow back
Yellow print	1 strip, 4" wide. Cut into 4 paths using Template B	Paths
Yellow print	Cut same strip to 3⅜" wide. Cut 4 paths using Template A	Paths
Golden yellow solid	2 strips, 1" wide. Cut into 4 lengths, 1" x 14½"	Flange
Pillow form	Use a pillow form 1" to 2" larger than the finished pillow for a fuller look	

Drunkard's Path Block Construction

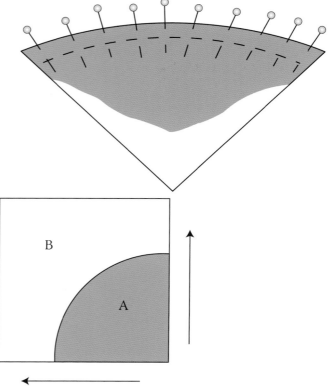

NOTE: *Two templates are used to construct the Drunkard's Path pattern; Template A is a convex curve, Template B is a concave curve.*

1. Fold the Template A pieces and Template B pieces in half to find the center of the arc; finger press or mark centers.

2. Place a Template A piece on the bottom and a Template B piece on top, right sides together. Match the centers, then outer edges, and pin. Continue to pin across the seam, clipping the concave curve as needed to ease across the convex curve. Sew carefully, open and press.

Drunkard's Path Pieces

3. Make four each of the Drunkard's Path combinations as shown.

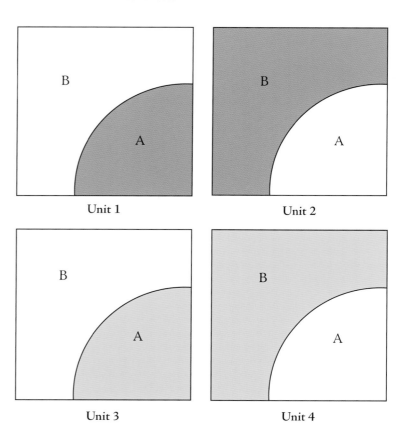

Unit 1

Unit 2

Unit 3

Unit 4

4. Sew two Unit 1 pieces and two Unit 2 pieces together as illustrated. Press.

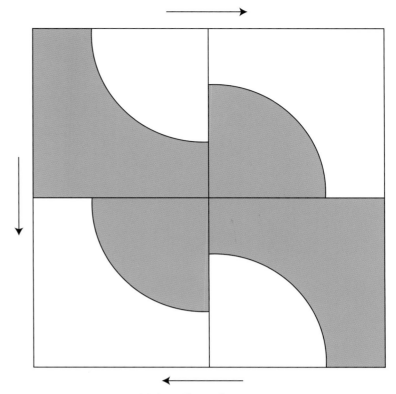

Make 2 Green Sections

5. Sew two Unit 3 pieces and two Unit 4 pieces together as illustrated. Press.

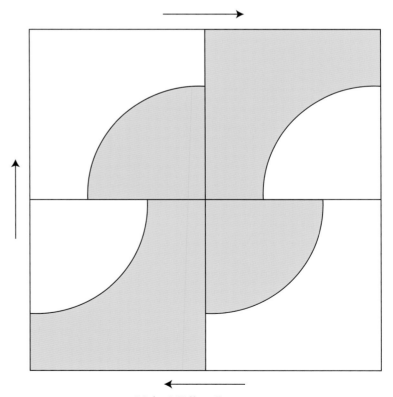

Make 2 Yellow Sections

6. Sew green sections and yellow sections together as illustrated.

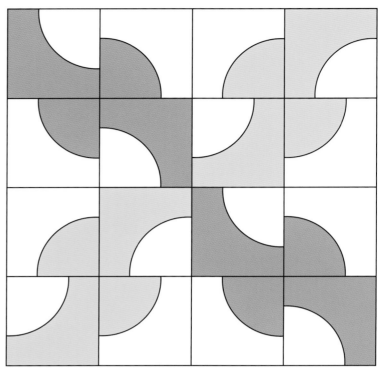

Drunkard's Path Block

Flange

1. Fold four of the 1" x 14½" flange strips in half lengthwise.

2. Place the raw edges of one strip along the top edge of the Drunkard's Path Block. Sew ⅛" from the edge. Repeat for the bottom edge.

3. Repeat by sewing two of the 14½" flange strips to the sides of the block.

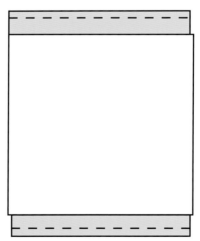

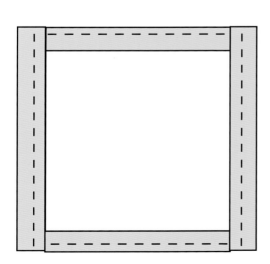

Borders

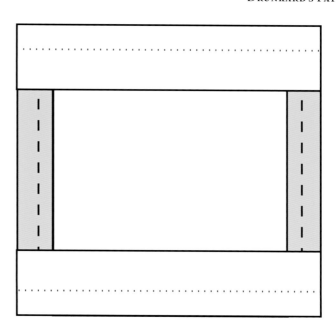

1. Cut one of the 2"-wide white strips into two 2" x 14½" lengths. Place the right sides together with the top and bottom of the pillow front, sandwiching the flange between the block and the border strips. Stitch along top and bottom of pillow front. Press seams toward outside.

2. Cut the remaining 2"-wide white strips into two 2" x 17½" lengths, and sew to the pillow sides. Press.

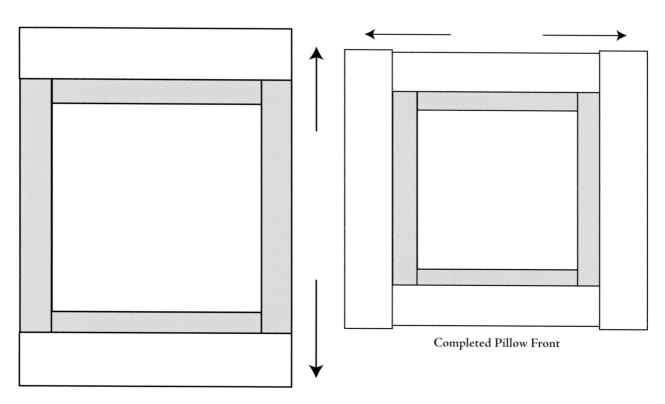

Completed Pillow Front

Pillow Construction

NOTE: *To make cording and construct the pillow, see Nine-Patch Novelty Print Pillow instructions.*

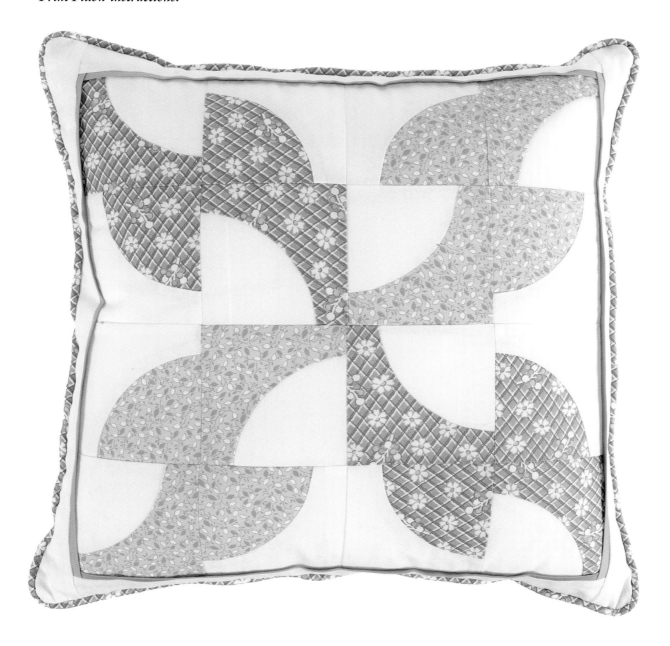

FAN DANCER QUILT

In the Fan Dancer Quilt, I modified the convex portion of the block by splitting it into two pieces. The sections "dance" with each other on a quilt that's a treat for the eyes!

Finished Quilt: 44" x 44"   Finished Block: 3½" x 3½"

Materials

1⅞ yd. black fabric
⅝ yd. yellow print fabric
⅜ yd. dark red fabric
⅜ yd. large red floral fabric
¾ yd. blue print fabric
2¾ yd. backing
50" x 50" batting
Sewing tools and supplies

Fabric	Cut	For
Black	8 strips, 4" wide. Cut 100 paths using Template B	Paths (see illustrations)
Black	15 strips, 1¾" wide	Border
Yellow print	2 strips, 3⅜" wide. Cut into 16 paths using Template A	Path
Yellow print	5 strips, 2¼" wide	Binding
Dark red	3 strips, 3⅜" wide. Cut into 36 paths using Template A	Paths
Large red floral	3 strips, 3⅜" wide. Cut into 36 paths using Template A	Paths
Blue print	3 strips, 3⅜" wide. Cut into 36 paths using Template A	Paths
Blue print	15 strips, ⅞" wide.	Border strips
Blue print	Cut one of the strips into 8 lengths, ⅞" x 5"	Corner units

Drunkard's Path Block Construction

Using Drunkard's Path Pillow instructions as a guide, sew all of Template A pieces to black Template B pieces. Make the number of blocks listed below.

- Yellow/Black: 16
- Blue/Black: 16
- Dark Red/Black: 32
- Large Red Floral/Black: 36

Quilt Assembly

Arrange the quilt pieces as illustrated, with 10 rows of 10 blocks each. Sew rows together; press seams away from the center row.

Borders

STRIP SET AND CORNER UNIT CONSTRUCTION

1. Sew the 1¾"-wide black strips and the ⅞"-wide blue print strips together as illustrated to make the border strip sets. Press.
2. Cut one of the strip set into 12 sections, 1¾" wide for the corner units.
3. Sew a ⅞" x 5" strip of blue print to each side of a 1¾" wide section to make Unit A. Press.
4. Sew a 1¾"-section to each side of a Unit A to complete the corner unit.

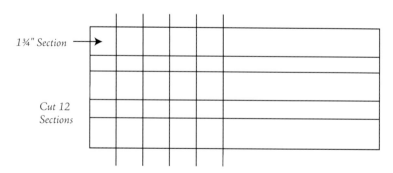

Black

Blue

Black

Blue

Black

Make 5

1¾" Section

Cut 12 Sections

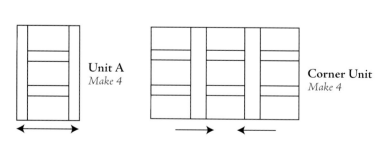

Unit A
Make 4

Corner Unit
Make 4

Border Placement

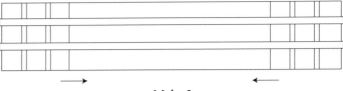

Make 2

1. Measure and cut the four remaining border strip sets to fit the top, bottom and sides of the quilt.
2. Sew border strip sets to the top and bottom of the quilt.
3. Sew a corner unit to each end of the two remaining border strip sets. Press. Sew to the sides of the quilt.

Finishing

Layer, quilt and bind. Refer to Finishing section in How-to Quilting Basics for detailed instructions.

FIREWORKS QUILT

The Fan Dancer and Fireworks quilts are constructed using the same fabrics. It is the layout that gives them their own distinctively different appearance. Plus, I added multi-colored thread to the Fireworks Quilt to make it look like fireworks are exploding.

Materials

1⅛ yd. black fabric
⅞ yd. dark red fabric
⅝ yd. yellow print fabric
¾ yd. blue print fabric
⅛ yd. gold print fabric
2¾ yd. backing
41" x 41" batting
Sewing tools and supplies

Fabric	Cut	For
Black	6 strips, 4" wide. Cut into 84 paths using Template B	Background paths
Black	2 strips, 4" wide. Cut into 16 paths using Template C, mark dots on fabric to match marks on template	Paths *(see illustrations)*
Dark red	5 strips, 3" wide	Strip set for circle section
Dark red	4 strips, 2¼" wide	Binding
Yellow print	6 strips, 3" wide	Strip set for circle section
Blue print	7 strips, 3" wide	Strip set for circle section
Gold print	1 strip, 2" wide. Cut into 16 paths using Template D	Paths

Modified Drunkard's Path Block Construction

1. Sew the red, yellow and blue strips together to make Strip Sets 1 - 3. Press.

Set 1
Make 2

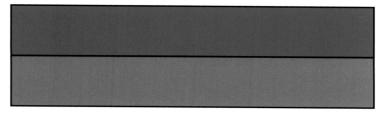

Set 2
Make 3

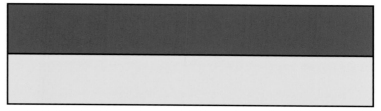

Set 3
Make 4

2. Lay Template A on top of each strip set, placing center line on the strip set seam. Cut to make the number of quarter-circle sections from each strip set as shown.

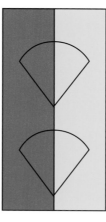

Set 1
Cut 16

Set 2
Cut 36

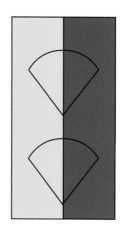

Set 3
Cut 48

3. Fold the Template A pieces and Template B pieces in half to find the center of the arc; finger press.

4. Place a Template A (red/blue quarter circle) on the bottom and a Template B on top, right sides together. Match the centers, then outer edges, and pin. Continue to pin across the seam, clipping the concave curve as needed to ease across the convex curve. Sew carefully, open and press. Sew a Template B piece to all 84 red/blue and yellow/blue quarter circles.

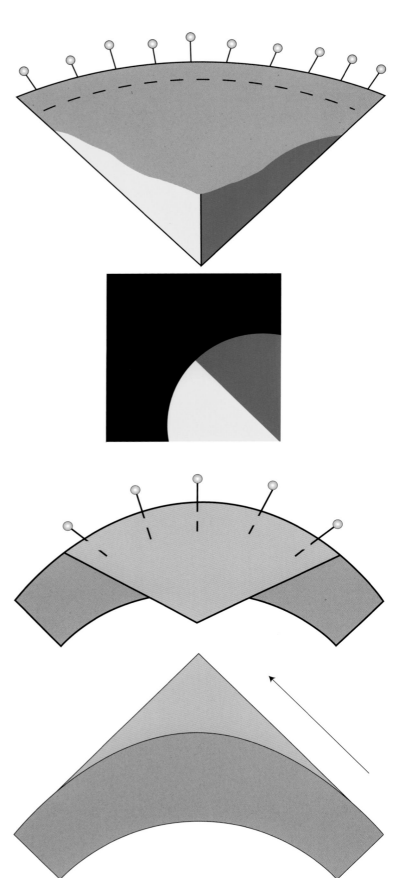

5. Fold a background Template C and a gold Template D in half to find the center of the arc; finger press.

6. Place a Template C on the bottom and a Template D on top, right sides together. Match the centers, then the dots, and pin. Continue to pin across the seam, clipping the concave curve as needed to ease across the convex curve. Sew carefully, open and press.

7. Sew 16 C/D Units to the 16 Red/Yellow of Template A as illustrated in directions for the 84 Template A and B sections.

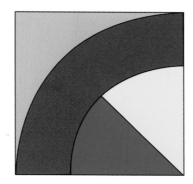

Quilt Assembly

Arrange the quilt pieces as illustrated with 10 rows of 10 blocks each. Sew rows together; press seams away from the center row.

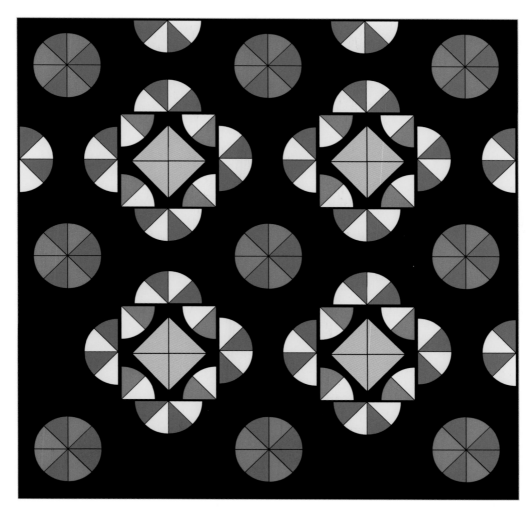

Finishing

Layer, quilt and bind. Refer to Finishing section in How-to Quilting Basics for detailed instructions. This quilt was quilted with multi-colored thread to make it appear that fireworks are exploding.

Finished Quilt: 35" x 35"   Finished Block: 3½" x 3½"

7

PINWHEEL FLOWER

I gave the quilts in this chapter a different look by using different size blocks and by using two completely different lines of fabric. The baby quilt was made using 1930's fabrics and the lap quilt is made with a purple monochromatic (one color) scheme.

Finished Quilt: 55" x 69"   Finished Block: 14"

PINWHEEL FLOWER LAP QUILT

When using a monochromatic scheme, use a variety of scales of print sizes and vary the light and dark colors.

Materials

1⅝ yd. cream print fabric
1½ yd. dark purple print fabric
1 yd. medium purple print fabric
½ yd. light purple print fabric
1¼ yd. large purple floral fabric
3¼ yd. backing
61" x 75" batting
Sewing tools and supplies

Fabric	Cut	For
Cream print	6 strips, 4" wide. Cut into 96 blocks using Template B	Background
Cream print	5 strips, 4" wide. Cut into 48 blocks using Template A	Background
Cream print	6 strips, 1" wide	Middle border
Dark purple print	10 strips, 4" wide. Cut into 96 blocks using Template A	Pinwheels
Dark purple print	6 strips, 1½" wide	Inner border
Medium purple print	3 strips, 4" wide. Cut into 48 blocks using Template B	Block corners
Medium purple print	7 strips, 2¼" wide	Binding
Light purple print	3 strips. Cut into 48 squares, 4" x 4"	Squares
Large purple floral	7 strips, 5½" wide	Outer border

Construction instructions to follow on page 108.

Finished Quilt: 39½" x 39½"   Finished Block: 10"

PINWHEEL FLOWER BABY QUILT

The traditional name of this quilt is "Windflower." I drafted the pattern from an old newspaper clipping that a student gave me. The clipping was dated 1932, and stated that readers could order the pattern for 10 cents in stamp or coin.

Materials

1 yd. cream solid fabric
⅜ yd. blue floral fabric
¾ yd. yellow plaid fabric
1⅛ yd. red bunnies fabric
¼ yd. dark blue fabric
1⅜ yd. backing
46" x 37" batting
Sewing tools and supplies

Fabric	Cut	For
Cream solid	4 strips, 3" wide. Cut into 72 of Template B	Background
Cream solid	3 strips, 3" wide. Cut into 36 of Template A	Background
Cream solid	1 strip, 2½" wide. Cut into 16 of Template D	Background
Blue floral	2 strips, 3" wide. Cut into 36 of Template B	Block corners
Blue floral	1 strip, 2½" wide. Cut into 16 of Template C	Outer border corner pinwheels
Yellow plaid	3 strips, 3" wide. Cut into 36 squares, 3" x 3"	Squares
Yellow plaid	5 strips, 2¼" wide	Binding
Red bunnies print	6 strips, 3" wide. Cut into 72 of Template A	Pinwheels
Red bunnies print	4 strips, 4½" wide	Outer border
Dark blue	4 strips, 1¼" wide	Inner border

NOTE: *Refer to the Hint for Perfect Narrow Borders in How-to Quilting Basics.*

Pinwheel Flower Block Construction

Note: *Piecing instructions are for both quilt sizes. Text and numbers in parentheses are for the Pinwheel Flower Baby Quilt.*

1. Fold the dark purple (red bunnies) of Template A and Template B pieces in half to find the center of the arc; finger press.

2. Place Template A pieces on the bottom and Template B pieces on top, right sides together. Match the centers, then the outer edges, and pin. Continue to pin across the seam, clipping the concave curve as needed to ease across the convex curve. Sew carefully, open and press. Make 96 (72).

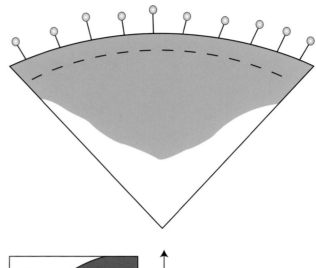

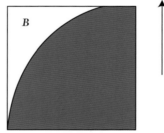

Unit 1

3. Fold a background of Template A and a medium purple of Template B in half to find the center of the arc; finger press.

4. Place Templates A and B right sides together. Pin and sew as directed in Step 2. Make 48 (36).

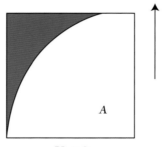

Unit 2

5. Sew Sections 1 - 4 together as illustrated. Press.

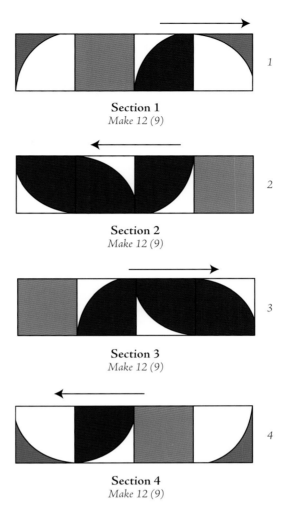

Section 1
Make 12 (9)

Section 2
Make 12 (9)

Section 3
Make 12 (9)

Section 4
Make 12 (9)

6. Sew Sections 1 - 4 together to make a Pinwheel Flower Block. Make 12 (9). Press.

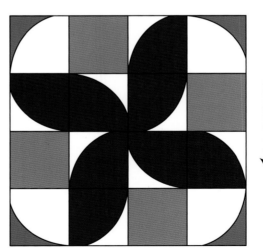

QUILT ASSEMBLY

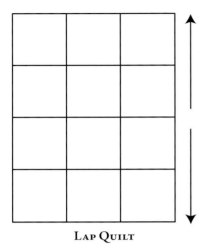

LAP QUILT

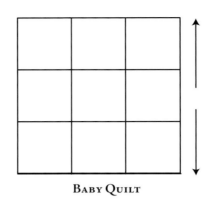

BABY QUILT

Arrange the quilt pieces as illustrated with 4 (3) rows of 3 blocks each. Sew rows together; press seams away from the center row.

Borders ~ Pinwheel Flower Lap Quilt

INNER BORDER
1. Measure, cut and sew three of the 1½"-wide dark purple print strips to the top and bottom of the quilt, piecing strips for needed length.
2. Repeat for the sides of the quilt.

MIDDLE BORDER
Repeat steps for Inner Border, using 1"-wide cream print.

OUTER BORDER
Repeat steps for Inner Border, using 5½"-wide large purple floral print.

Borders ~ Pinwheel Flower Baby Quilt

BORDER CORNER BLOCK

1. Fold a blue floral of Template C (concave curve) and the background of Template D (convex curve) of each fabric in half to find the center of the arc; finger press.
2. Place Templates C and D, right sides together, pin and sew as directed in the Pinwheel Flower Block construction. Make 16.
3. Sew together as illustrated.

INNER BORDER

1. Measure, cut and sew two of the 1¼"-wide dark blue strips to the top and bottom of the quilt.
2. Repeat for the sides of the quilt.

OUTER BORDER

1. Measure and cut two of the 4½"-wide red bunnies strips to fit the top and bottom of the quilt Do not sew to the quilt.
2. Measure and cut two of the 4½"-wide red bunnies strips to fit the sides of quilt. Sew a Pinwheel Corner Unit to both ends of the side border strips.
3. Sew top and bottom borders to the quilt.
4. Sew side borders to the quilt.

Finishing

Layer, quilt and bind. Refer to Finishing section in How-to Quilting Basics for detailed instructions.

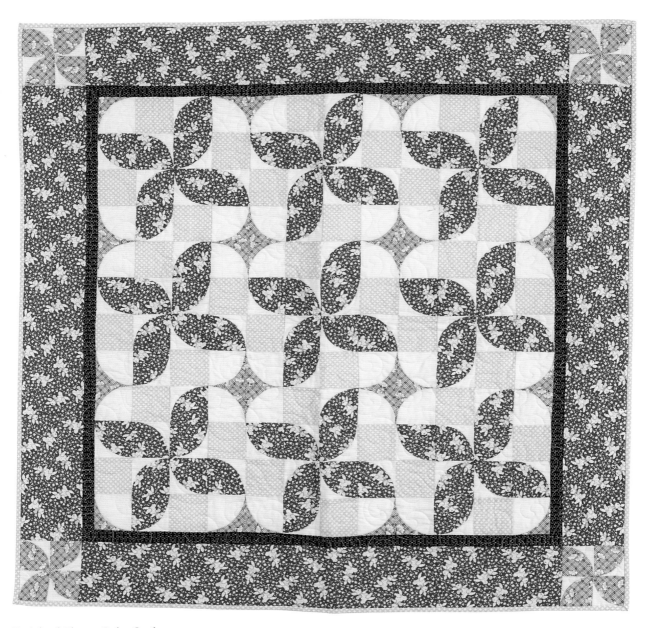

Pinwheel Flower Baby Quilt

Pinwheel Flower Lap Quilt

TEMPLATES

CHAPTER ONE TEMPLATES
FOUR RAIL FENCE BORDER APPLIQUÉ
Templates are drawn reversed for fusible appliqué.

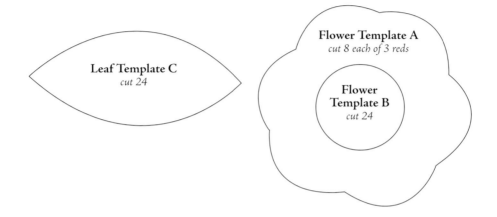

Leaf Template C
cut 24

Flower Template A
cut 8 each of 3 reds

Flower Template B
cut 24

CHAPTER TWO TEMPLATES
Country Log Cabin Border Appliqué
Templates are drawn reversed for fusible appliqué.

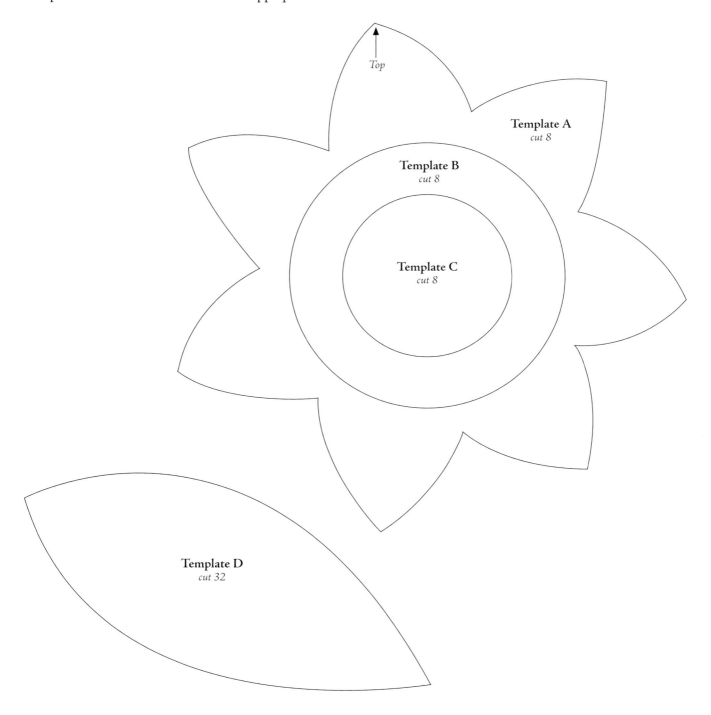

CHAPTER THREE TEMPLATES
PLACE MATS APPLIQUÉ
Templates are drawn reversed for fusible appliqué.

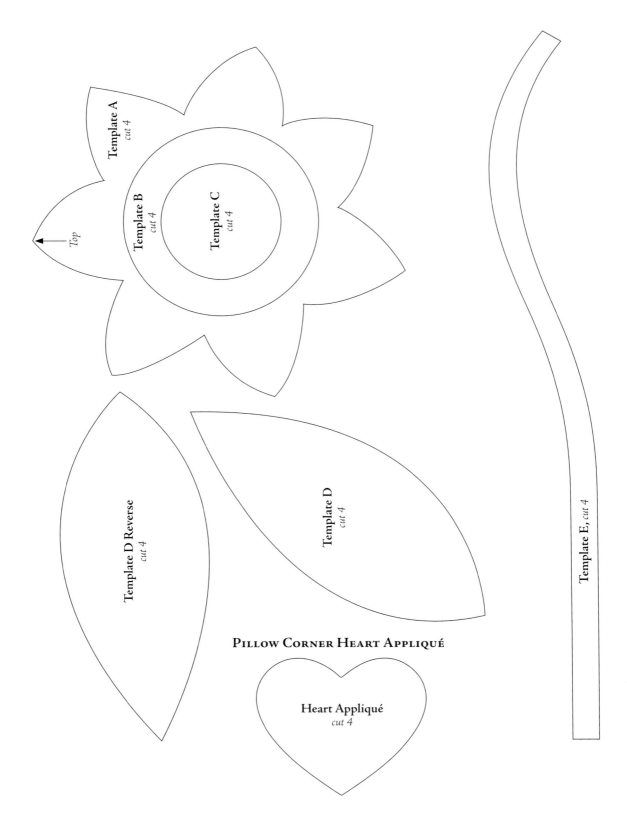

Template A *cut 4*

Template B *cut 4*

Template C *cut 4*

Top

Template D Reverse *cut 4*

Template D *cut 4*

Template E, *cut 4*

PILLOW CORNER HEART APPLIQUÉ

Heart Appliqué *cut 4*

CHAPTER FOUR TEMPLATES
NINE-PATCH BABY QUILT
Templates are drawn reversed for fusible appliqué.

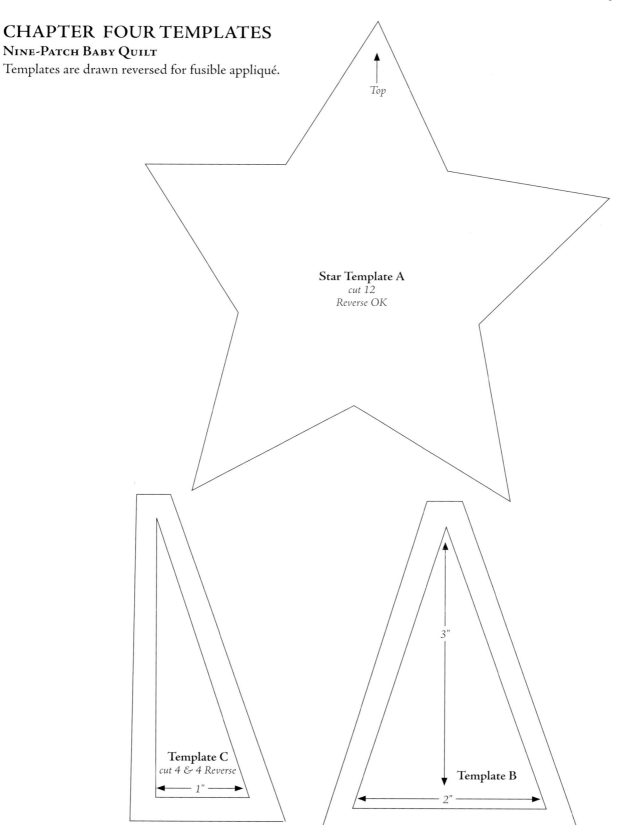

Top

Star Template A
cut 12
Reverse OK

Template C
cut 4 & 4 Reverse
← 1" →

3"

Template B
← 2" →

CHAPTER FOUR BABY QUILT
Nine-Patch

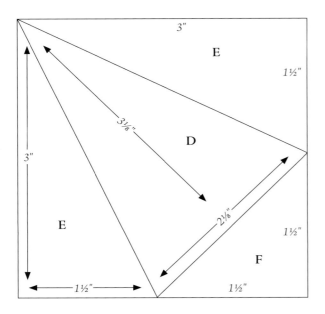

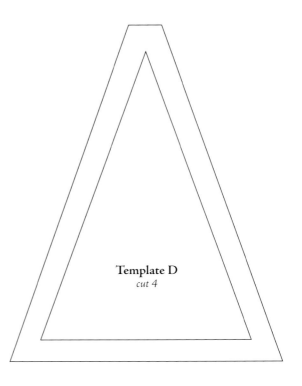

Template D
cut 4

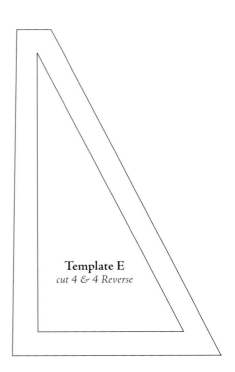

Template E
cut 4 & 4 Reverse

CHAPTER FIVE
WIND IN THE PINES

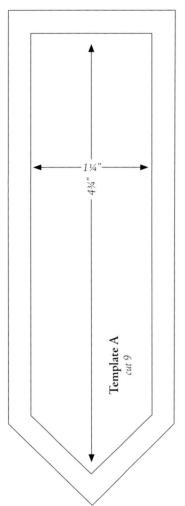

Tree Trunk

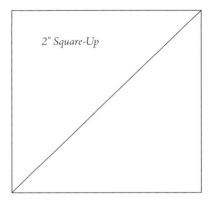

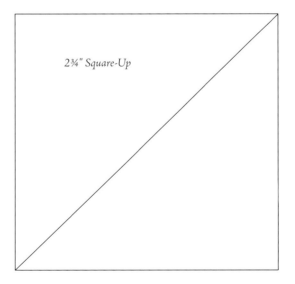

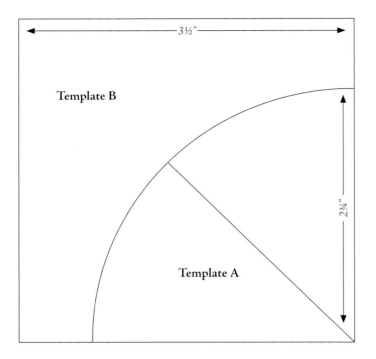

Template B

3½"

2¾"

Template A

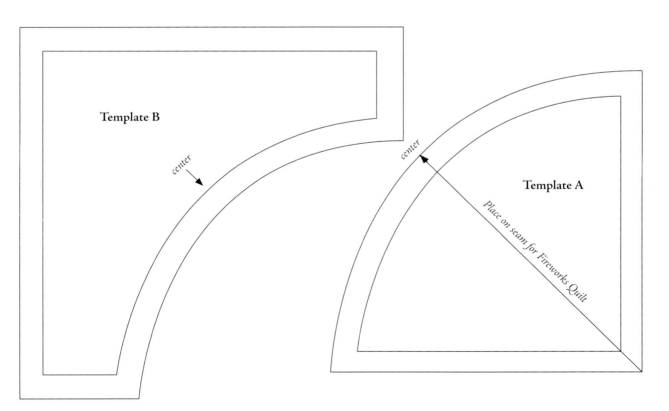

Template B

center

center

Template A

Place on seam for Fireworks Quilt

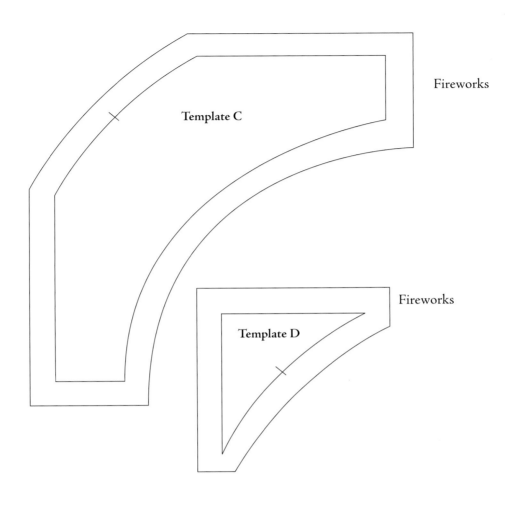

Fireworks

Template C

Fireworks

Template D

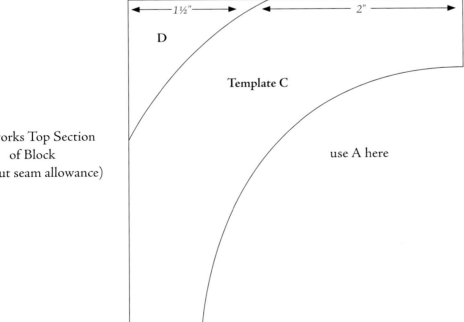

Fireworks Top Section
of Block
(without seam allowance)

1½"

2"

D

Template C

use A here

CHAPTER SEVEN
PINWHEEL FLOWER BABY QUILT

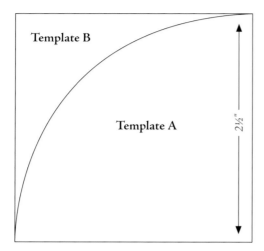

Template B

Template A

2½"

Baby Quilt Pinwheel
Flower Block
(seam allowance
not included)

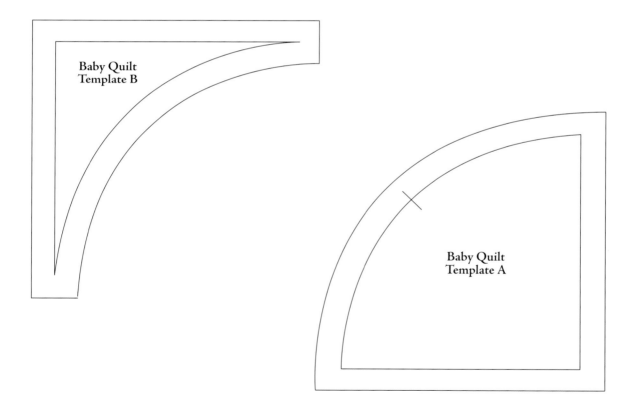

Baby Quilt
Template B

Baby Quilt
Template A

CHAPTER SEVEN
PINWHEEL FLOWER LAP QUILT

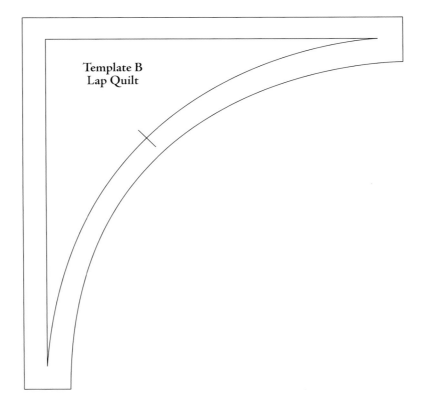

**Template B
Lap Quilt**

CHAPTER SEVEN
Pinwheel Flower Lap Quilt

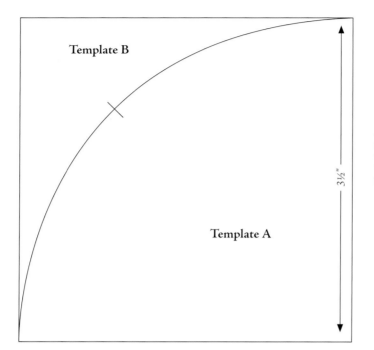

Template B

Template A

3½"

Lap Quilt Pinwheel
Flower Block
(seam allowance
not included)

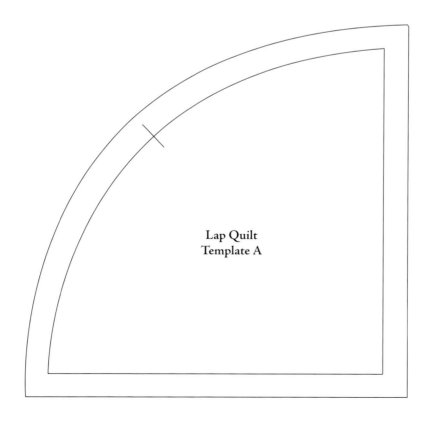

Lap Quilt
Template A

CHAPTER SEVEN
PINWHEEL FLOWER QUILT
BABY QUILT CORNER BORDER BLOCK

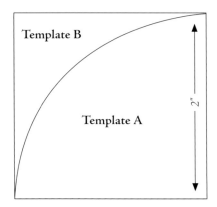

Template B

Template A

2"

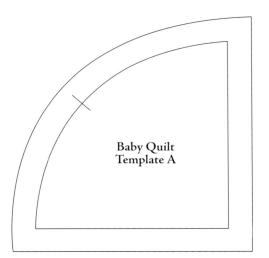

Baby Quilt
Template A

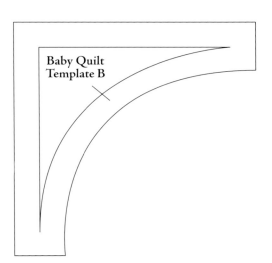

Baby Quilt
Template B

CONTRIBUTORS AND RESOURCES

ELISA'S BACKPORCH
Quarter Circle Templates
Drunkard's Path Templates
1200 Forest Road NW
Albuquerque, NM 87114
(505)-897-1894
www.backporchdesign.com

LEATH ENTERPRISES
Custom Templates
915-C West Foothill Blvd. #493
Claremont, CA 91711
(800)-515-4546, (909)-625-4546
E-mail: Rlea@msn.com
www.notions4less.com

PRYM CONSUMER USA, INC.
Omnigrid
P.O. Box 5028
Spartanburg, SC 29304
www.prymconsumerusa.com

SUPERIOR THREADS
P.O. Box 1672
St. George, UT 84771
(800) 499-1777
www.superiorthreads.com

JUST CURVES
2549-B Eastbluff Dr. #123
Newport Beach, CA 92660
949-721-0865
www.justcurves.com

THE WARM CO.
Insul-Bright™
954 E. Union Street
Seattle, WA 98122
(206) 320-9276
www.warmcompany.com

ADDITIONAL RESOURCES

ANNIE'S ATTIC
1 Annie Lane
Big Sandy, TX 75755
(800) 582-6643
www.anniesattic.com

CLOTILDE LLC
P.O. Box 7500
Big Sandy, TX 75755-7500
(800) 772-2891
www.clotilde.com

CONNECTING THREADS
P.O. Box 870760
Vancouver, WA 98687-7760
(800) 574-6454
www.ConnectingThreads.com

GHEE'S
2620 Centenary Blvd. No. 2-250
Shreveport, LA 71104
(318) 226-1701
E-mail: bags@ghees.com
www.ghees.com

HERRSCHNERS, INC.
2800 Hoover Road
Stevens Point, WI 54492-0001
(800) 441-0838
www.herrschners.com

HOME SEW
P.O. Box 4099
Bethlehem, PA 18018-0099
(800) 344-4739
www.homesew.com

KEEPSAKE QUILTING
Route 25
P.O. Box 1618
Center Harbor, NH 03226-1618
(800) 438-5464
www.keepsakequilting.com

NANCY'S NOTIONS
333 Beichl Ave.
P.O. Box 683
Beaver Dam, WI 53916-0683
(800) 833-0690
www.nancysnotions.com

YOU'LL NEVER RUN OUT OF FRESH IDEAS
WITH THESE GREAT BOOKS!

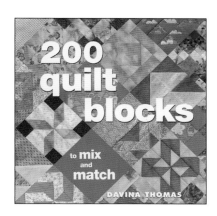

200 Quilt Blocks to Mix & Match
by Davina Thomas
eatures 200 contemporary and traditional quilt block designs, and step-
-step instructions to create more than 25 completed mix-and-match
ilts. Plus, a beautiful palette of 100 fabrics to refer to for making your
wn stunning pieces is included.

Softcover ♦ 8-¾ x 8-¾ ♦ 128 pages
200+ color photos
Item# QBMM ♦ $24.99

Quilted Bags & Totes
by Denise Clason
No matter what size you are, everyone can fit into a bag! Create stylish,
yet practical, bags including a backpack and makeup bag, using full-size
patterns.

Softcover ♦ 8-1/4 x 10-7/8 ♦ 128 pages
175+ color photos and illus.
Item# Z0106 ♦ $24.99

90-Minute Quilts
25+ Projects You Can Make in an Afternoon
by Meryl Ann Butler
Discover how easy it is to create stylish baby and large lap quilts, plus wall
hangings using the quick tips, methods and 250 how-to color photos and
illustrations included in this book.

Hardcover ♦ 8 x 8 ♦ 160 pages
250 color photos and illus.
Item# NTYMQ ♦ $24.99

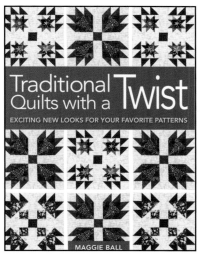

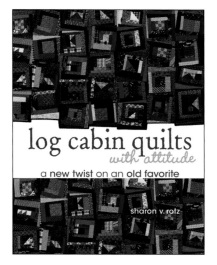

Traditional Quilts with a Twist
Exciting New Looks for your Favorite Patterns
by Maggie Ball
se traditional quilt blocks to create unique variations through more than
) projects demonstrated in 200+ color photos.

Softcover ♦ 8-¼ x 10-7/8 ♦ 128 pages
200+ color photos and illus.
Item# TRQV ♦ $22.99

Log Cabin Quilts With Attitude
A New Twist on an Old Favorite
by Sharon Rotz
Discover a new twist on traditional quilting, and showcase individuality
with the clever "freedom block" approach demonstrated in 15 step-by-step
projects and more than 250 color photos.

Softcover ♦ 8-¼ x 10-7/8 ♦ 128 pages
250+ color photos and illus.
Item# LCQA ♦ $22.99

Bundles of Fun
Quilts From Fat Quarters
by Karen Snyder
Perfect for fans of fat-quarter quilts and aspiring quilters alike, this book
provides fabric selection advice, instructions for making smaller quilts and
adding sashing and borders. Offers variations for 12 coordinating fabrics.

Softcover ♦ 8-¼ x 10-7/8 ♦ 128 pages
150+ color photos and illus.
Item# FQLQ ♦ $22.99

Krause Publications
Offer CRB6
PO Box 5009
Iola WI 54945-5009
www.krausebooks.com

To order call
800-258-0929
Offer CRB6

Please add $4.00 for the first book and $2.25 each additional
for shipping & handling to U.S. addresses. Non-U.S.
addresses please add $20.95 for the first book and $5.95 for
each additional.

Residents of CA, IA, IL, KS, NJ, PA, SD, TN, VA, and WI
please add appropriate sales tax.

TRADITIONAL TECHNIQUES FOR TODAY'S QUILTERS

Attic Windows
Quilts With a View, 2nd Edition
by Diana Leone & Cindy Walter
This timeless technique allows quilters of all skill levels to use creativity and favorite motif fabrics together. Includes information on selecting fabrics, tips on effective color usage, numerous exercises, and step-by-step instructions for one project.
Softcover ◆ 8¼ x 10⅞ ◆ 96 pages
100 color photos ◆ 20 illus.
Item# ATWI ◆ $19.95

Basic Applique
1930s Quilt Patterns Created With Traditional and Contemporary Techniques
by Cindy Walter & Gail Baker Rowe
This book teaches quilters six basic appliqué methods and provides 18 patterns from the 1930s. Includes easy-to-follow instructions, helpful hints and resources.
Softcover ◆ 8¼ x 11 ◆ 144 pages
120 color photos
Item# BGAPP ◆ $21.95

Everyone Can Quilt
with Kaye Wood
100+ Tips, Techniques, Templates & Projects
by Kaye Wood
Learn to quilt placemats, potholders, quilts, wall hangings and more quickly and easily! 24 projects use rail fence, pinwheel, 9-patch and star patterns.
Softcover ◆ 8¼ x 10⅞ ◆ 144 pages
75 color photos ◆ 300 illus.
Item# EOCQ ◆ $22.99

Granny Quilts
Vintage Quilts of the '30s Made New for Today
by Darlene Zimmerman
This full-color pattern book offers 19 projects for creating quilts that replicate the look of the popular quilts of the 1930s. Features a variety of pieced and appliquéd quilts.
Softcover ◆ 8¼ x 10⅞ ◆ 128 pages
70 color photos & 65 illus. ◆ 25 full-size templates
Item# GRANQ ◆ $21.95

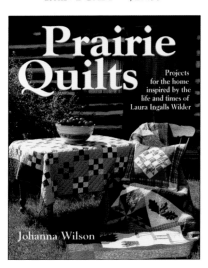

Prairie Quilts
Projects for the Home Inspired by the Life and Times of Laura Ingalls Wilder
by Johanna Wilson
Relive the pioneer era with these 20 gorgeous projects reminiscent of the beloved stories of Laura Ingalls Wilder. Author Johanna Wilson guides all skill levels through the projects, while illustrating their relationship to the Wilder books and sharing her private collection with readers.
Softcover ◆ 8¼ x 10⅞ ◆ 128 pages
100 color photos ◆ 250 illus.
Item# PRQD ◆ $21.99

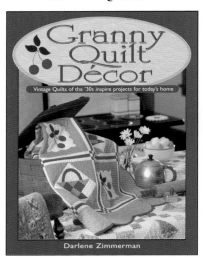

Granny Quilt Décor
Vintage Quilts of the '30s Inspire Projects for Today's Home
by Darlene Zimmerman
Features quilting ideas for all skill levels, including bed-sized quilts, wall hangings, pillows, kitchen novelties and more. Includes more than 30 fantastic projects and basic quilting instructions, as well as a fascinating historical look at these '30s era quilts.
Softcover ◆ 8¼ x 10⅞ ◆ 128 pages
125 color photos ◆ 150 illus.
Item# GQDCR ◆ $21.99
